FireStarter

The Holy Spirit Empowers

By Philip J. Noordmans

2

Table of Contents

4

Foreword

Usually books on the Holy Spirit have good theology and biblical teaching, but render the Third Person of the Trinity impersonal, dull, and dry. They do not draw us into the author's lived experience. Or, they are full of exciting experiences with the Holy Spirit, but they do not help us build a good biblical and theological foundation for understanding and cooperating with the Holy Spirit. This book is a masterpiece of doing both. As you read, you will grow in personal experience as well as biblical understanding!

For me, reading this book was a great blessing. Even though I have taught on the Holy Spirit for many years through Presbyterian Reformed Ministry International's (PRMI's) Dunamis Project, still Phil's work led me into a deeper understanding of the biblical teaching on the Holy Spirit. I will need to go back and rewrite some of our teaching materials to include Phil's insights.

I am deeply honored that the author refers back to my own teaching on the Holy Spirit, as well as to experiences that he had at various Dunamis Project equipping events. In this book, Phil has done for me what the Lord called me to do for my own mentor and teacher, Archer Torrey. That is, he has taken PRMI's teaching on the Holy Spirit, and by the leading of the Holy Spirit, filtered it through the lens of his own experience and personality, refining it and improving it. As a result, Phil equips us personally and academically to build up others. We are drawn together into an amazing dance of cooperating with the Holy Spirit that is advancing the Kingdom of Jesus Christ to the glory of God the Father.

Rev. Dr. Zeb Bradford (Brad) Long
Executive Director
Presbyterian Reformed Ministries International

Let the Adventure Begin!

Scores of people from around the world are experiencing the Holy Spirit working in their lives in dynamic ways. The purpose of this book is not to say – or even suggest – that I can top their stories. Rather, my contribution is to humbly offer a practical understanding of the empowering work of the Holy Spirit that is rooted in Scripture and illustrated by His work in my life and the lives of others.

What we believe matters. Beliefs form the foundation for behaviors, and right beliefs lead to righteous behaviors.

A few years ago Marcus Yoars observed,

> We have a generation dangerously close to losing grasp of the fundamental principles of what being filled with the Holy Spirit is all about. I pray we see a renewed commitment from leaders to preach and teach on why the baptism of the Spirit matters more now than ever.[1]

By God's grace He is leading me – academic, reserved, Bible-believing me and hundreds like me – on a path that sets the

---

[1] Marcus Yoars, 10 Revolutions for the New Year - Charisma Magazine, Dec. 18, 2012), 6.

heart to singing! Central to the journey is a Biblically balanced understanding of the Person and work of the Holy Spirit.

A.W. Tozer noted that,

> In most Christian churches, the Spirit is quite entirely over-looked. Whether He is present or absent makes no real difference to anyone. Brief reference is made to Him in the doxology and the benediction. Further than that He might as well not exist. ... Our neglect of the doctrine of the blessed Third Person has had and is having serious consequences. For doctrine is dynamite. It must have emphasis sufficiently sharp to detonate it before its power is released. ... The doctrine of the Spirit is buried dynamite. Its power awaits discovery and use by the Church. ... The Holy Spirit cares not at all whether we write Him into our creeds in the back of our hymnals; He awaits our emphasis.[2]

Let the adventure begin!

---

[2] A.W. Tozer, *Tozer on the Holy Spirit: A 366-Day Devotional Compiled by Marilynne E. Foster*, 2007).

PART I: MY STORY BEGINS

Chapter 1: It Didn't Add Up

Phil Noordmans
Age 2

The distance between the corn crib and the machine shed was about fifty steps. But the encounter with the Holy Spirit that occurred in that small space on our family's dairy farm in west-central Minnesota frightened me. Suddenly, distinctly, a strange jumble of sounds (words?) exploded in my eleven-year-old head. Bewilderment turned quickly to fear and in the name of Jesus I rebuked the devil. In time the "language" stopped.

My father was a strong church-going, Bible-believing Christian who learned dispensational theology from Scofield-trained preachers. Dispensationalists believe that "sign gifts" such as prophecy, miracles, and tongues ceased with the close of the New Testament canon. At some point during my teenage years, dad told me a story about one of his experiences as a young man in the Navy. His ship docked at an island – I believe it was Guam. He and a buddy went ashore and found a church. During the worship service someone spoke in tongues. Following the service dad's buddy told my father that he understood the tongues-speaker's language and that he was praising the devil. From that time on dad held firmly to the conviction that "all tongues-speaking is of the devil" – a conviction that he passed on to me.

Donnie puzzled me. He seemed so normal! Donnie managed a successful nursing home facility in Evansville, Indiana. He attended Christian Fellowship Church where I served on staff from 1975-1980. He loved to hunt and so did I, and that's where our paths crossed. Over time we developed a friendship. One day Donnie shared with me in a matter-of-fact manner that he spoke in tongues. Further, he testified that at one time he had a serious knee problem that needed surgery. While watching TV one evening the preacher invited people with physical problems to put their hands on their television sets in their living rooms, believe God for a miracle, and receive prayer for healing. Donnie did – and was miraculously healed!

It didn't add up. Donnie's story rocked my worldview. Normal Christians are not supposed to speak in tongues, and miracles of healing are not supposed to happen in our day – certainly not through wacked-out TV preachers! Even though I had been taught that tongues and miracles ceased with the close of the New Testament canon, Donnie seemed so credible. It didn't add up.

In 1978, the senior pastor of Christian Fellowship Church, three elders, and I sat in Charlie's comfortable living room sipping hot tea and discussing "speaking in tongues." The issue had surfaced in our church and as leaders we needed to agree on the position we would present to the congregation. After a couple hours of thoughtful conversation, we moved into a time of prayer, and that's when it happened. For the first time that I can recall God spoke directly to me. Three words thundered into my mind: JESUS IS LORD!

In early 2000, as I sat studying in my office at Faith Reformed Church, Traverse City, Michigan, Sharon walked in and handed me a very simple, non-professional looking, three-fold brochure. "Read this," she said, "and pray about attending." The brochure sat on my desk for 2-3 weeks before I got around to reading it, but when I did, I learned that it was an invitation to attend a Dunamis Conference at Maranatha Bible and Missionary Conference Center in Muskegon, Michigan, sponsored by a team of people associated with Presbyterian Reformed Ministries International (www.prmi.org). As I studied Brad Long's picture on the front of the flyer and read his brief bio, the Holy Spirit whispered to my inner man, "You need to spend time with Brad." I made arrangements to attend. Life has never been the same.

Over time, I learned that Presbyterian Reformed Ministries International, headquartered in Black Mountain, North Carolina, is a ministry committed to teaching about the Person and work of the Holy Spirit from a Reformed theological perspective. Practically, what that means is this:

- On one end of a continuum, we find faithful Christians from Pentecostals and Assembly of God backgrounds who trust in Jesus Christ, are born again, and believe that the only evidence of baptism with the Holy Spirit is speaking in tongues.

- On the other end of this continuum, we find genuine, Christian dispensationalists who believe that all manifestational gifts ceased with the close of the New Testament canon.

- Somewhere in the middle lives PRMI.

In time, by God's grace, I transitioned from being one of the people attending PRMI's semi-annual Dunamis Conferences to one of the people in leadership. This wonderful journey with the Holy Spirit and with good friends continues to this day.

As a result of careful study and dynamic experiences, I am convinced that all the spiritual gifts mentioned in Scripture are available to Jesus' followers in our day. (Yes, there are also abuses.) Speaking in tongues is an evidence of baptism with the Holy Spirit but not the evidence. Rather, it is one of several possible confirmations of the Holy Spirit's empowering work in a person's life.

It didn't add up, but now it does.

Chapter 2: Deep Cleaning, Deep Healing

Before Jesus will use a person in His service, He must do
house cleaning – often deep cleaning, and inner healing. The
more Jesus intends to use a person, the deeper He will
clean. Self and sin must go. Truth and light must be welcomed
to heal and renew.

Most of us include "confession of sin" as one of our regular
spiritual disciplines. What follows is a deeply personal
description of a time in my life when Jesus accomplished a
needed work of grace in my heart.

Journal Entry, May 8, 2002. Maranatha Conference Center,
Muskegon, Michigan. PRMI's Dunamis Project on "The
Healing Ministry of Jesus."

> God has given Susan,[3] a member of the prayer team,
> eyes to see into my soul! It is almost unnerving. After
> she discerned that the Adversary had robbed me of my
> confidence to function as a man and as a leader in the
> roles to which God is calling me, and that the root of
> the problem had something to do with my relationship
> to my earthly father and mother, she suggested that we

---

[3] While the stories in this book are true, names and identifying information
may have been changed to protect the privacy of individuals.

meet with Mr. and Mrs. Chan for a time of prayer. God orchestrated the events of the evening so that at 10:30 p.m., five of us were available to meet in a side room. Our prayer session lasted for two intense hours and I wish I could remember the full sequence of events and details of the encounter. All I know is that within minutes after we met, I began to experience deep, deep, grief – a grief that swallowed my voice and produced tears that flowed freely down my face.

At some point in the session, Susan said, "Phil, I am going to address you as your mother." Then, with God's help she spoke precious affirmations to me as if I were her little boy, telling me how proud she was of me and what delight I brought to the family dinner table as well as to other aspects of life. She asked for forgiveness for waiting so long to tell me of her love for me, and her joy in me. Through Susan's words my soul heard my mother's voice. I grieved the losses and began to heal as I stammered through my tears, "Mom, I forgive you."

At another point, Richard addressed me as my father. Once again, assisted by the Holy Spirit, his voice became the voice of my father. In that role, Richard asked for my forgiveness for several failures and I was able to forgive my dad.

Mr. and Mrs. Chan led me to renounce the enemy's strongholds in my life and to put on the full armor of God for spiritual protection, applying the blood of Christ to all aspects of my life. They led me to affirm that I am a man whom God created with strengths and gifts to be used to advance the Kingdom of God.

As our time together drew to a close, they anointed me with oil. Then, they prayed blessing upon Teri (my wife), myself, our marriage, our family, and our ministries.

What a night! I praise God for His deep cleaning, for His patience with me, for His care for me, and for His power to bring inner healing, setting this captive free!

We cannot manufacture or orchestrate seasons of deep cleaning in our own lives, or as much as we might like to, in the lives of others. Jesus schedules them in His appointment book. Our initial response may be one of reluctance and resistance. However, when we look back on the experience we will recognize it for what it truly is – a mercy-filled gift from God – and we will give thanks with grateful hearts.

Walk With Me

In 1997, on a damp, bone-chilling, northern Michigan morning, I pulled on a warm coat, boots, and gloves and went out for a walk in the hills near our home in Traverse City. As I reached a plateau and ambled forward I "heard" a distinct "voice" invite (or, was it a command?), "Walk before me."

Since then, in obedience to that invitation, I have prayer-walked many, many miles with the Father, Son, and Holy Spirit. And the journey continues.

Woven throughout the ups-and-downs of real life – family problems, church challenges, and financial decisions – is a growing relationship with the Holy Trinity.

Walk with me. Let the adventure – your adventure – begin!

For Further Reflection

In Chapter 1, "It Didn't Add Up," and Chapter 2, "Deep Cleaning, Deep Healing," I described several memorable, personal, experiences. What are some parallels between my story and your story?

PART II: GETTING TO KNOW THE HOLY SPIRIT

Many times I begin my prayer walk saying, "Good morning, Father, Son, and Holy Spirit." I have not always done this. For much of my life my interest pertained to what the Holy Spirit could do for me – e.g., produce love in my heart and give wisdom in difficult situations – rather than in having a relationship with Him similar to our relationship with the Father and the Son.

Striving to develop a deeper relationship with the Holy Spirit inevitably leads to a deeper relationship with Jesus Christ because the Holy Spirit deflects attention from Himself to Jesus.

He will glorify Me. John 16:14, ESV

Chapter 3: Who the Holy Spirit Is

One of the questions that people around the world are asking is, "Who is the Holy Spirit?" According to Google AdWords, every month 673,000 people search online for the answer to this question.

In a word, the Holy Spirit is the third Person in the Trinity. He is God, He is holy, He is a Person, and He is powerful! He is not our equal or our servant, but our Sovereign Lord.

1. The Holy Spirit is a Person who may be grieved.

> Do not grieve [4] the Holy Spirit of God, by whom you were sealed for the day of redemption. Ephesians 4:30, ESV

The Holy Spirit is a Person with feelings and emotions. He loves us, and we can grieve our lover. The Holy Spirit is not an "it" or a "thing" or an impersonal "force" as in Star Wars, "The force be with you." Rather, He is a Person. We cannot have a relationship with a bicycle, a frying pan, a tree, or the wind, but we can with a person.

---

[4] Unless otherwise noted, underlining has been added for emphasis.

He is "grieved" or "saddened" when we:

- Ignore Him.
- Pursue other lovers.
- Value our relationships with other people more than we value our relationship with Him.

The Prophet Isaiah pointed to the serious consequences that may befall those who grieve the Holy Spirit when he wrote,

> *In his love and in his pity he redeemed them;*
> *he lifted them up and carried them all the days of old.*
> *But they rebelled*
> *and grieved his Holy Spirit;*
> *therefore he turned to be their enemy,*
> *and himself fought against them.*
> Isaiah 63:10-11, ESV

Fortunately for us, in His mercy Jesus draws near to forgive us when we sincerely repent.

2. The Holy Spirit is a Leader who may be resisted.

Stephen angered the religious leaders in his day when he exclaimed,

> *You stiff-necked people, uncircumcised in heart and ears, you always resist the Holy Spirit."* Acts 7:51, ESV

The Holy Spirit is a Leader who has plans and purposes. In ordinary terms, "He is a Man with a plan." We resist the Holy Spirit when we put our agenda on a higher peg than His. We resist the Holy Spirit when we know what He is nudging us to do but refuse to do it.

In my journal I made the following notation:

> During our communion time at a Dunamis event (May 2005) I sensed Jesus whisper a word to my heart saying, "My son, you are forgiven." For me, that was huge. Why? Because three or four times during the previous evening [Saturday evening] I missed Holy Spirit "nudges" and I knew it. For example, when the prayer team gathered prior to the evening meeting to be anointed with oil for the ministry time that would follow, I expected Jon be there and lead but he had been pulled aside into a deliverance ministry session. As a result I was in charge but I was unprepared. Time was short, so to save time I suggested a plan: "I will anoint Judy who in turn will anoint Tom …." The moment I said those words, I received a "message" in my spirit – "No, I was to anoint each person." But I ignored it and pressed forward with my plan.

> Later that evening following a wonderful time of worship I sensed that the Spirit had drawn near and was ready to work among us. However, the next thing on our agenda was a PRMI report from Jeannie. Again I ignored the Spirit's whisper. I followed our agenda and turning the microphone over to Jeannie. As soon as I did, I knew that I had resisted and grieved the Holy Spirit again.

> Later, during prayer ministry, I sensed that Kate was to pray with one of the ladies in the back of the room. Instead, I asked Dawn to minister to her and sent Kate to another lady.

By the end of the evening I went back to my room feeling very empty. I took a walk, reflected, and confessed my willfulness.

That's why God's whisper to me during the communion time, "My son, you are forgiven," was so extraordinarily meaningful. The burden of guilt lifted. I could begin again anew. Due to His grace I could make a fresh start.

A few weeks later I made another notation in my journal:

I was praying with the healing prayer team today for Marcie. Before we began to pray I quietly promised the Holy Spirit that I would speak forth any words He revealed to me. During the course of that 30 minute season of prayer, I had 2-3 opportunities to choose either the path of obedience or shrink-back in doubt. In this case, by God's grace, I chose the path of obedience and walked away feeling that I had done my part and that the rest was up to God.

The mindset that leads to the good life is this:

Today, if you hear his voice, do not harden your hearts. Hebrews 4:7, ESV

Dance with the Holy Spirit! Let him lead the dance … and sense His pleasure.

3. The Holy Spirit is a powerful Person, but He is not a bully.

Do not quench the Spirit! 1 Thessalonians 5:19, ESV

The Holy Spirit is powerful, but He is not a bully. Generally, He will not force Himself upon us. Rather, He does His best work when He is welcomed.

Do not quench the Spirit. To "quench" something is to diminish it. On one occasion, when starting a fire in the fireplace in our home, I added too much dry kindling too quickly and the fire flamed-up very hot very fast. To quench the fire, I threw a little water on it. The water did not totally extinguish the fire – we cannot "kill" the Holy Spirit – but dampened it.

Do not quench the Spirit. When the Holy Spirit is burning hot, let Him burn! When He is doing a good work in someone's life, let Him work! Do not suppress, stifle, or hinder His activity in your life or in others.

There have been times in my life when I have quenched the Spirit. One Sunday night, for example, I attended an area praise gathering. Toward the end of the evening, the Pastor called the prayer teams to come to the front and then he invited attendees go forward for prayer. I went and received prayer from one of the couples. At one point in the prayer process, they paused and the lady asked, "Are you having a problem with your left leg?" I said, "No."

In reality, I was not having a "problem" with my left leg but at that moment it was shaking and quivering almost uncontrollably. By choosing to not tell the lady what I was experiencing, I believe that I quenched the Spirit. In other words, I believe that I hindered the work that Jesus would have done in my life that night if I had simply admitted, "At the moment my leg is really quivering and shaking."

Developing a relationship with the Holy Spirit, and surrendering to Him, often results in His power being released to work in us, and through us. R.A. Torrey wrote:

> While the power [of the Holy Spirit] may be one kind in one person and of another kind in another person, there will always be power. The very power of God, when one is baptized with the Holy Spirit.[5]

In future chapters we will say more about "baptism with the Holy Spirit."

Who is the Holy Spirit?

- The Holy Spirit is a Person. Do not grieve Him.
- The Holy Spirit is a Leader with an agenda. Do not resist Him.
- The Holy Spirit is a powerful Person, but He is not a bully. Do not quench His working in your life or in your fellowship.

---

[5]See R.A. Torrey, *Power-Filled Living* (New Kensington, PA: Whitaker House, 1999), 216.

Chapter 4: Developing Intimacy with the Father, Son, and Holy Spirit

In March, 2013, I sensed Jesus calling me to deeper intimacy with Himself. Honestly, my first response was, "Jesus, I'm not sure I want to go there because I'm not a touchy-feely sort of guy. Further, it sounds to me like You are calling me to spend less time doing what I want to do (my priorities; my agenda) and more time with You."

Several years ago I heard someone define intimacy as "into me see." That's a good definition but it is one-sided. In the process of mulling over Jesus' invitation it occurred to me that true intimacy with God flows in two directions:

- God sees into my heart. I open myself to Him, hiding nothing. I give Him total access to every room in my "house."

- I see into God's heart. Jesus opens a window to His heart and lets me take a look inside. This understanding is based on Jesus' decision to call us "friends" and to make known to us what He is hearing from the Father (see John 15:14-15).

Eventually I came to realize that by calling me into deeper intimacy with Himself, God was inviting me to see and to know Him – to see what He sees when He looks at broken lives of needy people in our hurting world as well as at His bride, the Church – and to hear His longings, plans, dreams, and desires for us.

A few days ago I was on a three-way call with Nick and Jim. As we prayed about a conference that would begin the following week – a conference entitled "Growing the Church in the Power of the Holy Spirit," I sensed in my spirit that we were approaching a "veil" that, at the moment, was drawn. I sensed that if it were drawn back by the Divine Hand, we would be allowed a glimpse into God's plans for the people who would be participating in that conference. Unfortunately we became distracted and failed to linger in that holy moment and hence missed what He had for us.

As intimacy with our Triune God deepens, with greater frequency He draws us to the edge of the unseen realm. In His good time He draws back the veil to reveal what lies ahead and how we are to cooperate with Him.

That's a sacred trust! Who wouldn't want that?!?

Gardening Together for Life: A Metaphor for Growing Intimacy

> Once upon a time, there lived a wealthy man – whom we will call Gordon – who owned a large garden. Gordon loved growing beautiful and fruitful things in his garden. People who knew him called him "Gordon the Gardener." Gordon's garden was gigantic, like an arboretum. Roses and shrubs; apricot trees and tomato plants; watermelons, summer squash, and more.

Even though Gordon the Gardener loved to garden and was able to take care of the entire garden by himself, he decided to hire an apprentice. He interviewed several applicants and in due time chose a young man named Albert. People who knew him called him "Albert the Apprentice."

When Albert first came to work in Gordon's garden, they had a master-servant relationship. Each day began with Gordon the Gardener telling Albert the Apprentice what to do that day and how to do it. Albert did just what Gordon instructed him to do, nothing more, nothing less.

For several months, Gordon the Gardener watched Albert the Apprentice and noticed that he was a faithful and obedient servant. Further, Gordon noticed that Albert had developed a knack for gardening. He, too, was good at helping things grow.

One day, Gordon called Albert to join them on the patio for a cool glass ice tea. "Albert," Gordon began, "I've been watching you work and you are learning our trade well. Up to this point I have told you what to do each day and you have done it. Good work! But it's time for a change. When you come to work tomorrow, I want you to tell me two or three things that you see that need to be done in my garden. We will discuss your ideas, and if they fit with my bigger plans for the garden, we will work together to implement your ideas."

And that is what happened. Gordon the Gardener remained ultimately in charge, but from that day forward Gordon and Albert worked together like partners and friends in Gordon's garden.

Jesus said to His disciples,

> *You are my friends if you do what I command you. No longer do I call you servants, for the servant does not know what his master is doing; but I have called you friends, for all that I have heard from my Father I have made known to you.* John 15:14-15, ESV

Servants do not know their Master's business. They do not know His desires or His plans for the present or for the future. Nor do they know His heart.

But friends do. Intimacy is the Gardener's gift to His friends.

Jesus' invitation in John 15 is not addressed to scribes and Pharisees. Nor is it addressed to people who spend most of the day and half the night cultivating their own gardens. Rather, Jesus' invitation to friendship – to intimacy – is limited to servants who obey all His commandments, especially His command to love one another as He has loved us.

Living Life as Jesus' Friends

For Jesus' servants, communication flows one way: from the top down. For Jesus' friends, communication flows two ways: from heaven to earth and from earth to heaven.

> *You did not choose me, but I chose you and appointed you that you should go and bear fruit and that your fruit should abide, so that whatever you ask the Father in my name, he may give it to you.* John 15:16, ESV

Jesus' friends engage their Master in prayer and combine their prayers with fitting works. In the process the Garden grows both beautiful and fruitful.

- The garden will always belong to Gordon the Gardener.
- Albert will always be a servant working in Gordon's Garden.
- But the important shift is this: Albert is now a servant who is a friend. Now Gordon and Albert work together as partners tending Gordon's Garden.

Now, that's rewarding!

Chapter 5: What the Holy Spirit Does

The purpose of this chapter is to provide an introduction to several of the key ways that the Holy Spirit works in our lives today. In the chapters that follow we will weave together teaching and story to draw us toward a balanced understanding of, and experience of, one of the Holy Spirit's overlooked and often misunderstood works, namely, His marvelous grace of empowerment.

"Empowerment" is one slice of a much bigger pie. The Holy Spirit not only convicts, regenerates, adopts, seals, teaches, intercedes, guides, and sanctifies; He also *empowers* people for greater witness and service.

In the Old Testament, the Spirit came "upon" a few, select individuals empowering them to do mighty works and/or speak anointed words. In the New Testament, in fulfillment of Joel's prophecy, the Holy Spirit hovers near every Christian ready and willing to come "upon" them, equipping and empowering each one to join the dance of cooperation with the Father, Son, and Holy Spirit. As a result we too will be enabled to dynamically participate in fulfilling our mandate in Acts 1:8 of being witnesses in our Jerusalem, Judea, Samaria, and world. Our "personal Pentecost" empowers and releases us to be even more effective as the Lord's servants.

THE HOLY SPIRIT'S ROLE IN OUR GREAT SALVATION

A. PRE-CONVERSION WORKS OF THE HOLY SPIRIT

1. The Holy Spirit convicts of sin

I thank God for the Holy Spirit's convicting work in my life because it led me to repentance and faith in Jesus. I will share that story in a moment.

Shortly before His crucifixion Jesus said to His disciples,

> *Nevertheless, I tell you the truth: it is to your advantage that I go away, for if I do not go away, the Helper will not come to you. But if I go, I will send him to you. And when he comes, he will <u>convict</u> the world concerning sin and righteousness and judgment.* John 16:7-8, ESV

A few months later, on the Day of Pentecost (Acts 2), the Holy Spirit demonstrated His ability to convict people of sin. Luke recorded the audience's response to Peter's sermon by saying,

> *Now when they heard this they were <u>cut to the heart</u>, and said to Peter and the rest of the apostles, "Brothers, what shall we do?"* Acts 2:37, ESV

2. The Holy Spirit works with the Father to draw people to Jesus

> *No one can come to me unless the Father who sent me draws him.* John 6:44, ESV

Methodists talk about "prevenient grace." John Wesley described prevenient grace as the work of the Holy Spirit wooing us toward a relationship with Jesus. Prevenient grace prevents us from moving so far from the path of life that our hearts become hardened. When we finally hear the gospel, we are prepared to say "Yes." In comparison, "justifying grace" pertains to our conversion and "sanctifying grace" to the Spirit's work of transforming us from the inside-out to make us more like Jesus Christ.

My Journey to Jesus

I grew up in rural, west-central Minnesota. In many ways I lived the normal life of a middle child in a family of seven on a dairy farm – driving tractors, milking cows, doing chores, hunting, fishing, playing with my cousins, going to school, and attending church. Even though my dad kept me too busy to get into much trouble, I grew up with the awareness that I had done lots of little things wrong. I felt guilty. I felt like something wasn't quite right between me and God.

When I was around 11 years old, our family piled into our 1955 Studebaker on a Monday evening and drove to our little church to hear a guest preacher, a wiry man who declared with great fervor that the communists were going to take over the United States by 1975, and when they did, they might start killing people. One of his questions was, "Are you ready to die?"

As I listened to that man's crazy message – "crazy" is my adult assessment of what he was teaching – I was scared on two levels:

- Human level. Remember, I was only 11 years old, and I did not want a big, bad communist killing me or my family!

- Spiritual level. Deep within I knew that I was not ready to die because I had done things wrong. God is holy, and I was not ready to stand before Him and be examined by Him.

The preacher invited people to walk to the front during the last hymn, repent of their sins, put their faith in Jesus Christ, and receive from Jesus forgiveness and new life. Deep within, my heart said, "I want that; I need forgiveness and new life." But I resisted the Holy Spirit's convicting work in my heart. Well do I remember sitting in the back row with my buddies and gripping the pew's edge so hard that my knuckles turned white. I was not going to make a fool out of myself by walking to the front!

On Tuesday evening, our family returned to church. Same preacher. Same sort of sermon. Same conviction – only this time, stronger. By God's grace I humbled myself and yielded to the Holy Spirit's call, walked to the front, knelt down, confessed my sins to Jesus, and asked Him to come and live in me.

I remember walking out of that little church into the cool, Minnesota evening, looking up at the star-filled night sky and feeling lighter than air! Even though I was only 11 and could not have done that many things wrong, I felt like a big load had been lifted from my shoulders. The guilt was gone and I felt free! I knew that I was right with God. I knew I was ready to die. Even more, I knew that I was ready to live.

B. THE HOLY SPIRIT'S ROLE IN OUR CONVERSION

Marvel at the Holy Spirit's involvement in our great salvation!

When we repent of our sins and place our faith in Jesus Christ, Jesus applies His blood to the doorposts of our hearts and we experience our spiritual birthday. The Father justifies us (justification) by God's grace through the redemption that is in Christ Jesus (Romans 3:24; Galatians 3:24) and sends the Holy Spirit to live in us (John 14:16-17). Jesus said,

> *I will ask the Father, and he will give you another Helper to be with you forever, even the Spirit of truth, whom the world cannot receive, because it neither sees him nor knows him. You know him, for he dwells with you and will be in you.* John 14:16-17, ESV; cf. 1 Corinthians 6:19

The same thing that happened to the 11 apostles when Jesus breathed on them and said, *Receive the Holy Spirit,* (John 20:22, ESV) happens to us.[6] We are *born again* (John 3:5-7) by

---

[6] Cf. Galatians 3:1-2; Romans 8:13-16; 1 Thessalonians 4:8

the Spirit. He gives us new life (John 6:63) and adopts us into God's family (Romans 8:15-16).

Paul taught clearly that,

> *Anyone who does not have the Spirit of Christ does not belong to him.* Romans 8:9, ESV

Further,

> *The Spirit himself bears witness with our spirit that we are children of God.* Romans 8:16, ESV

At the time of our conversion, the Holy Spirit also seals us, guaranteeing that we belong to Jesus (Ephesians 1:13-14). Further, He baptizes us into the body of Christ (1 Corinthians 12:13); that is, He places us into the body of Christ, and gives us spiritual gifts (Romans 12:6-8). Through faith in Jesus Christ, we are born again and incorporated into the Kingdom of God.

C. POST-CONVERSION WORKS OF THE HOLY SPIRIT

Following our conversion, the Holy Spirit continues to be very active in our lives. Let's take a look at five dynamic dimensions of the Holy Spirit's post-conversion work.

1. The Holy Spirit transforms us (sanctification; character development).

As soon as the Holy Spirit takes up residence within us, He begins His work of transforming us from the inside-out, making us more and more like Jesus Christ (2 Corinthians

3:18; Romans 15:16). The character qualities of Jesus Christ, also known as the fruit of the Spirit (Galatians 5:22-23; Luke 10:21; 1 Thessalonians 1:6), begin to develop within us. As we cooperate with Him, the Holy Spirit slowly but surely transforms us into people who are more loving, joyful, peaceful, patient, kind, good, faithful, gentle, and self-controlled.

I thank God for His steady work of transformation, through the Holy Spirit, within me!

In Scripture sanctification has past, present, and future dimensions. Here is an overview of these dynamics:

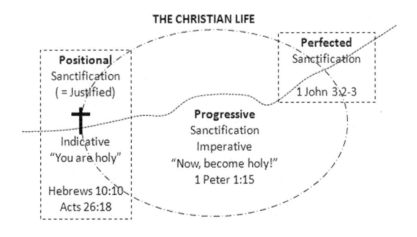

THE CHRISTIAN LIFE

The Apostle Paul intertwined the Holy Spirit's marvelous works of regeneration, renewal, justification, and glorification into one sentence when he wrote,

> *But when the goodness and loving kindness of God our*
> *Savior appeared, 5 he saved us, not because of works*
> *done by us in righteousness, but according to his own*
> *mercy, by the washing of regeneration and renewal of*
> *the Holy Spirit, 6 whom he poured out on us richly*
> *through Jesus Christ our Savior, 7 so that being*
> *justified by his grace we might become heirs according*
> *to the hope of eternal life.* Titus 3:4-7, ESV

2. The Holy Spirit walks with us (companionship).

Many people struggle with feelings of loneliness and isolation. On occasion I have felt lonely on the beach, in a crowded shopping mall, and even in our marriage. A few days ago I met a student from China who was studying in San Diego, California. After informing me that he had been in America for only one week, he said, "I am feeling lonely." On another occasion, a brilliant PhD student from China told me that her long hours of work in the lab left her feeling alone and lonely. Sailors also struggle with loneliness, and so do their families who are left behind when they deploy.

God created us to feel the emotion of loneliness so that we will long for companionship, not just earthly companionship with family, friends, and pets, but soul-satisfying companionship with God Himself through the Person of the Holy Spirit. For lonely people the good news is this:

> *I will ask the Father, and he will give you another*
> *Helper to be with you forever, even the Spirit of truth,*
> *whom the world cannot receive, because it neither sees*
> *him nor knows him. You know him, for he dwells with*
> *you and will be in you. I will not leave you as orphans;*
> *I will come to you.* John 14:16-18, ESV

Even though we cannot see Him or touch Him, the Holy Spirit is present to provide companionship for those who will pursue a relationship with Him by means of classic spiritual disciplines, such as meditating on Scripture, prayer (yes, we may address the Holy Spirit in prayer), fellowship, and worship. Let this be one of our prayers:

> "Holy Spirit, we want to know You. We hunger for a deeper, soul-satisfying relationship with You. Teach us how to walk through each day – including this day – heart-to-heart and hand-in-hand with You."

John Adams (1735-1826) observed, "You will never be alone with a poet in your pocket." We have Someone who is better by far than a poet. Our companion is the Holy Spirit.

3. The Holy Spirit manifests His presence among us, that is, in our midst.

On a Sunday morning, following a brief time of worship at a Dunamis event at Lake Ann, Michigan, in May 2002, I directed the 17-18 people who were present to find a quiet place around the retreat center and ponder Acts 13. They did. Eventually we re-gathered, shared thoughts from our time alone with Jesus in His Word, and began Communion.

The evening before, the Lord had prompted me to ask William – an ordained minister who was attending the conference – to lead the Communion time. He asked if he could invite his friend Jean – also an ordained minister – to assist.

William began by reading from Isaiah 55 and from the Beatitudes, focusing on "hunger" and "thirst." He tied these words into Lake Ann Camp's repeated refrain, "Nobody,

nobody, at Lake Ann Camp goes hungry. There's more
through the door!" "Jesus," said William, "is the door and He
always has more for His children."

Then, William invited Jean to consecrate the elements. Jean
stepped forward and began. Speaking softly and clearly,
moving gracefully, and looking each participant in the eye, she
recited the words of institution. Beautifully done.

Following Communion, Ruth said, "May I say something?"
She proceeded to report that when Jean looked at her, she did
not see Jean but Jesus! Ruth said, "I almost fell to my knees."
Then four or five others in the group reported brief stories of
remarkably deep things God had done in them while Jean was
consecrating the elements. For example, Kathleen said, "When
you said that Jesus invites people from the North and South,
East and West, to join Him at table, my heart leapt for joy! My
family is from the East." Dawn tearfully testified that she had
been feeling very weary for several weeks, and that Jesus said
to her, "I know your weariness and I will give you rest." Even
Tucker reported tears, saying, "I'm an emotional rock; I never
cry."

The Spirit of God manifested His presence in our midst and we
were deeply touched.

The Holy Spirit not only works in individuals; he also works
within groups. The opening chapters in the Book of Acts
introduce us to the corporate dimension of the Holy Spirit's
activity.

> *Suddenly there came from heaven a sound like a mighty
> rushing wind, and it filled the entire house where they
> were sitting.* Acts 2:2, ESV

When they had prayed, the place in which they were gathered together was shaken, and they were all filled with the Holy Spirit and continued to speak the word of God with boldness. Acts 4:31, ESV

In another setting the Apostle Paul may have been referring to something that a group experienced together when he wrote,

And we all, with unveiled face, beholding the glory of the Lord, are being transformed into the same image from one degree of glory to another. For this comes from the Lord who is the Spirit. 2 Corinthians 3:18, ESV

The point is that the Holy Spirit not only works in us but also among us. On occasion He manifests His presence among us, and when He does, profound things result.

Following a Dunamis Fellowship meeting (January 2012) at Blue Ridge YMCA in Black Mountain, North Carolina, I journaled the following:

Toward the end of our Thursday evening's session the Lord gave someone the guidance that we were to stand together in one large circle. We did, waiting quietly before the Lord. From deep within my spirit came the cry, "Fire! Fire, fall!" I said nothing out loud but a few moments later the Holy Spirit fell powerfully upon PRMI's Executive Director, Brad Long. While functioning under the anointing of the Holy Spirit he invited everyone to join him in the center of the circle. As we did he called out the names of people and countries [Example: Where's Phil? We've got to pray for China.] As Brad laid hands on people, the Holy Spirit gloriously fell upon them. Some rested in the Spirit. Others wept; some laughed joyfully; others quietly received what God had for them. Clearly this powerful and refreshing anointing came to equip us to minister in the Spirit's power for Jesus' glory to the nations. What a remarkable launch of the Dunamis Institute! We are crazy enough to believe that God will work through ordinary people like us to impact the nations.

R.A. Torrey told a story that reveals the transforming power that results when the Holy Spirit works corporately among His people. Ministers in the Chicago area were daily holding noon prayer meetings in the YMCA in preparation for a series of meetings led by Mr. Moody. During one of the prayer meetings, a Baptist minister sprang to his feet and said, "Brother Torrey, what we need here in Chicago is an all-night prayer meeting of the ministers." Torrey willingly agreed and invited the pastors to meet at Moody Church the following Friday at 10 P.M.

On that Friday evening, six or seven hundred ministers and other Christian workers, both men and women, gathered for prayer. Initially the devil attempted to spoil the meeting. For example, three men began to shriek, shout, and pound their fists in prayer. When someone rebuked them for being disorderly they swore at him. A little later another man sprang to his feet and proclaimed that he was Elijah. By this time some of the more timid people in the prayer meeting decided to go home but the bulk of participants determined to stay. Torrey reported,

> About midnight God gave us complete victory. All the discordant elements were eliminated; and oh! what praying there was from that time on up to a little after two in the morning. I think I had never heard such praying before and have seldom heard such praying since. At 2:13 (I know the time, for I had taken out my

watch a few moments before), we were all on our knees, and suddenly the Holy Spirit fell upon us. No one could speak, no one could pray, no one could sing. All you could hear was the subdued sobbing of joy unspeakable and full of glory. It seemed to me as I knelt there that if I had looked up I would fairly have seen the Holy Spirit in that place.[7]

The ripple effect of that corporate encounter with the Holy Spirit reverberated for years. For example, the following week a business man traveled to Missouri. After transacting his business, we went to a nearby Presbyterian church where they were holding a meeting and asked if he could say a few words. Since he was well known in that denomination they said, "Yes." He poured out his soul to the congregation and fifty-eight people were converted.

Torrey concluded by saying,

As I went around the world in 1902 and the years that followed, in pretty much every field that I visited, Japan, China, New Zealand, Australia, England, Scotland, and Ireland, and other lands, I met with men or women who had gone out from that meeting with the power of God resting upon them.[8]

Suffice it to say that when the Holy Spirit shows up in the midst of His people, remarkable things happen! There will be lasting fruit for the Kingdom of God, fruit that is consistent with Scripture and gives glory to Jesus Christ.

---

[7] R.A. Torrey, *The Holy Spirit: Who He Is and What He Does* (Classic Books for Today, NO. 152, 2000), 50-51.
[8] Ibid.

4. The Holy Spirit flows through us.

On the last day of the Feast of Tabernacles, Jesus stood and cried out with a loud voice,

> *"If anyone thirsts, let him come to me and drink. Whoever believes in me, as the Scripture has said, "Out of his heart will flow rivers of living water." Now this he said about the Spirit.* John 7:37-39, ESV

Living water is life-giving water. The Holy Spirit is the *Living Water* who flows into us when we are born again, and then through us to bring new life to others. When we live our lives in cooperation with God, we become conduits of the Holy Spirit's regenerating power.

A young man named Jay shared the following story:

> In September, 2012, as I was getting gas on the north side of Grand Rapids, a large African American man holding a gas can approached me and asked for a dollar. I heard the Lord telling me to give him a $20 bill, and so I did. He was amazed and thanked me. As he slowly walked away I asked him if I could ask him a question. Eagerly he agreed. I knew what the Lord was guiding me to ask even though he was a pretty big dude. But because God is for us and not against us, I knew I could step out and ask it. "If you were to die today, would you go to heaven or hell?"
>
> "Sir, I can see you are a man of God," was his response.
>
> "Yes," I nodded.
>
> He looked down. "I'd go to hell."

Then he gave me a summary of the poor choices he had made during his life. I paid for my gas and he asked for a ride to his car. I heard the Lord's "go-ahead" and invited him into my car with me. This felt a little intimidating due to his size. He was a former semi-pro football player and I'm pretty sure he must have played offensive guard!

While we drove, I continued sharing the gospel with him starting with Adam and Eve in the Garden of Eden.

Was it my best presentation ever? No, it wasn't. But everything I said was true and God used it. The experience really reminded me of the verse from Zechariah 4:6, *It's not by might, nor by power, but by my Spirit says the Lord.*

When I asked if he wanted to give his life to Jesus, he said, "Yes." We prayed together and he surrendered to Jesus as Lord and Savior. When I asked him how he felt after praying, he said, "I have more peace." He looked much better physically!

I gave him a Bible and my card to keep in contact. I also encouraged him to begin to ask God what needed to change in his life so he could walk closer with Jesus.

5. The Holy Spirit comes "on" or "upon" us (empowerment).

In a 2007 edition of Newsweek magazine, author and radio personality Garrison Keillor was asked to choose what he considered to be the five most important books ever written. Some readers were probably surprised to find that he ranked the Book of Acts at the top of his list. When describing it, Keillor offered this concise but potent summation:

> "The flames lit on their little heads and bravely and dangerously went they onward."[9]

The fifth dimension of the Holy Spirit's work points to Pentecost (Acts 1:5-8; 2:1-4), to that remarkable day when the disciples were baptized with the Holy Spirit and thereby empowered for more effective witness and service. I will have much more to say about this.

In January, 2013, as I prepared to teach at our church on "Winning Life's Battles," I had a sense that God intended to call someone from among us to serve as a high-level intercessor, engaging and defeating dark angels. On Sunday, toward the end of the message, I identified three levels of pray-ers. The third level pertained to "spiritual warfare pray-ers." As I moved into that phase of the teaching, the Spirit of the Lord fell strongly upon me, very strongly. As is often the case when that happens, I had difficulty speaking. Yes, it is a little embarrassing to stand before a congregation and not be able to speak for several moments.

My guess is that most people in the congregation simply concluded that for some reason I was feeling emotional. However, I knew that I was experiencing something far deeper than human emotion. I was trembling; I was shaking; and, I believe that the Holy Spirit was at work at that moment to accomplish His divine purposes. Eventually the Lord helped me compose myself enough to make the point and conclude the service.

---

[9] Garrison Keillor, "My Five Most Important Books" (*Newsweek Magazine*, December 2007), 17.

Although I do not know for sure, I have an idea who the Lord was calling to serve as a high-level prayer warrior and I am waiting for her to come to this realization. It may be weeks, even months, before God's word bears fruit. God's timing is always best.

As an interesting aside, following the service no one asked me what was going on in me during the sermon. I don't blame them. Ten to fifteen years ago, I would have responded in the same way. Displays of God's presence and power can be so unsettling and so "out-there" that the average church-goer chooses to overlook them. But I remain in awe of God.

That's one illustration of the empowering dimension of the Holy Spirit's work. Here is another.

While serving Communion to our congregation in San Diego in March, 2014, I stood behind the altar as I usually do while the Deacons passed the elements. During that quiet moment a phrase totally unrelated to the theme for the morning came to mind: "Blessed are the pure in heart for they shall see God." Although I was not 100% sure why that phrase came to mind, I decided to take it as a word from the Lord and share it with the congregation. After all, what is the worst that could happen? Hence, at the conclusion of the Communion service I said, "As the elements were being passed today, the phrase, 'Blessed are the pure in heart for they shall see God' came to mind. That may be for someone here today. You have been seeking God, and He will show up."

As we moved from worship to our fellowship lunch, I essentially forgot about that statement until Linda stopped me and said excitedly, "Pastor Phil, that was for me!" She proceeded to explain that she had been praying during communion about a complicated political situation regarding her teaching role at a university. "I've been asking Jesus to mentor me. Jesus used your words to encourage me deeply."

Jesus works through men and women who are empowered by the Holy Spirit to advance His agenda.

> *YOU will receive power when the Holy Spirit has come upon you!* Acts 1:8, ESV

> *The promise is for you and for your children and for all who are far off, everyone whom the Lord our God calls to himself.* Acts 2:39, ESV

Summation

An awareness of these interconnected spheres of operation of the Holy Spirit gives us a foundation for understanding not only Biblical references to the Holy Spirit, but also personal experiences with the Holy Spirit. He works in us, with us, among us, through us, and upon us.

The empowering work of the Holy Spirit will be described and illustrated in more detail in the chapters that follow. Stay tuned and read on with expectation …

For Further Reflection

Chapter 3: Who the Holy Spirit Is

1. Talk about times in your life when you may have grieved, resisted, or quenched the Holy Spirit.

2. Ask Jesus to forgive you for your lack of sensitivity to, and lack of cooperation with, the Holy Spirit. Recognize that self-serving actions and attitudes will always hinder the Holy Spirit. Invite Jesus to deepen your desire to grow in intimacy with the Father, Son, and Holy Spirit.

Chapter 4: Developing Intimacy with the Father, Son, and Holy Spirit

1. How has your relationship with the Holy Spirit developed during recent years?

2. What are your longings in your relationship with the Trinity? Use words to paint a picture of a relationship with the Father, Son, and Holy Spirit that is steadily growing deeper and stronger.

Chapter 5: What the Holy Spirit <u>Does</u>

1. Reflect on your journey to Jesus, and share some of your memories with the group.

2. Give thanks to the Father, Son, and Holy Spirit for specific ways that They have been at work in your life personally and in your fellowship gatherings.

3. What hungers or longings are being birthed in your heart by the Holy Spirit?

PART III: THE SPIRIT IN THE OLD TESTAMENT

The New Testament's understanding of, and experience of, baptism with the Holy Spirit (i.e., empowerment) is rooted deep in the soil of the Old Testament. We will see that, in most cases, when the Spirit came "on," "upon," or "clothed" a person, he was empowered <u>to do mighty works</u> and/or <u>to speak anointed words,</u> and we will point out aspects of the Spirit's empowering work in the Old Testament that continue into our day. Our insights will emerge from a study of the Spirit's work in the lives of five men: Gideon, Samson, King Saul, Amasai, and David.

Chapter 6: The Spirit Empowered Gideon

Gideon: Historical Context

The Book of Judges is an account of the life and times of twelve men and women who served as "Judges" during a desperate phase in the history of the nation of Israel, c.1380 BC – 1050 BC (about 330 years). The first Judge began to serve shortly after Joshua died, and the last Judge (Samuel) walked off the stage of history shortly after he anointed Saul and David to serve as Israel's first and second kings.

Who or what was a "Judge"? A good way to answer that question is to make a few comparisons.

- The function of a "governor" is to lead the state.
- The function of a "mayor" is to lead a city.
- The function of a "general" is to lead an army.
- The function of a "judge" was to lead the nation of Israel. Judges provided primarily military and civil leadership in Israel.

The Bible states clearly that the Spirit of the Lord came "upon" or "clothed" four of the twelve Judges referenced in the Book of Judges empowering them to advance God's agenda. In each case, the result of the Spirit's empowerment was dynamic action. Dr. Thomas Constable observed succinctly, "When

God's Spirit came on individuals in the Old Testament, He empowered them for divine service."[10]

Gideon's Transformation

Gideon was not a natural leader. Rather, he was a poor farmer's son (Judges 6:2,11) who struggled with low self-esteem. When the angel initially approached him, Gideon said in essence, "God, you have dialed the wrong number."

> *Please, Lord, how can I save Israel? Behold, my clan is the weakest in Manasseh, and I am the least in my father's house.* Judges 6:15, ESV

Nevertheless, God had something He wanted done, and for reasons known only to God, he chose Gideon to do it. Realizing that timid Gideon needed special help, God clothed Himself with Gideon – yes, you read that correctly – thereby equipping Gideon to succeed.

In the story of Gideon, the primary statement pertaining to empowerment occurs in Judges 6:34. Translators phrase it as follows:

- *So the Spirit of the Lord came upon Gideon.* Judges 6:34, NAS
- *Then the Spirit of the Lord came on Gideon.* Judges 6:34, NIV
- *But the Spirit of the Lord clothed Gideon.* Judges 6:34, ESV

---

[10] Dr. Thomas Constable commenting on Matthew 3:17.
http://www.soniclight.com/constable/notes/pdf/matthew.pdf

54

According to the Hebrew lexicon edited by Brown, Driver, and Briggs, we are to translate Judges 6:34 as follows: *and the Spirit of God clothed itself with Gideon*. The lexicon goes on to say that "G.F. Moore understands this to mean that the Spirit of God 'took possession of him.'"[11]

"Clothed Himself With Gideon"

Let's think this through. We put on clothing. Our clothing does not go into us; rather, it rests on or upon us. Clothing is not internal but external. The man Gideon was like an external article of clothing.

The Holy Spirit is a spirit: He does not have a body. Hence, in order to accomplish the work He wants done and speak the words He wants spoken, the Spirit needs a human body – in this case, Gideon's. God's Spirit clothed Himself with Gideon. The Spirit is the One who is putting on the cloak, and the cloak He is putting on is a person – Gideon. Apparently, the Spirit moved from heaven above, came down upon Gideon, entered into him, and took control of him.

Result: Gideon was empowered by the Spirit. Gideon's mind, voice, and hands became the tools that the Spirit of God used to accomplish His work.

Imagine that happening to you! And you have a foretaste of Pentecost.

---

[11] Bauer, Arndt, Gingrich, *A Greek-English Lexicon of the New Testament and Other Early Christian Literature* (Chicago, IL: The University of Chicago Press, Thirteenth Impression, 1971), 528. The same statement is used to describe the Spirit's work in Amasai (1 Chronicles 2:18) and Zechariah (2 Chronicles 24:20).

Significantly, Jesus referred to this concept following His resurrection and prior to Pentecost:

> *Behold, I am sending the promise of my*
> *Father upon you. But stay in the city until you*
> *are <u>clothed with power</u> from on high.* Luke 24:49, ESV

If a candle represents the life of an ordinary person who is submitted to God and cooperating with God, then a torch represents the life of a man or woman who is being empowered by the Spirit of God. A candle is good, but during times of special need a torch is better by far.

Some of us, like Gideon, are not natural leaders but we are committed to following Jesus. What if God caused the candle of our lives to periodically flame-up like a torch?!?[12]

That is what happened to Gideon and, in New Testament terms, that is what happens to us when the Holy Spirit comes upon us and clothes Himself with us. For a few moments in time, the candle of our lives becomes a torch, and God accomplishes His extraordinary work through ordinary people like us.[13]

Let this be one of our prayers during times of need:
"Holy Spirit, cloth Yourself with me!"

---

[12] That is what happened to me during the worship service that I mentioned earlier. The Holy Spirit clothed Himself with me, and the words that people heard come out of my mouth were really from God's heart. Jesus, through the Holy Spirit, was doing His work through me.

[13] In future chapters, we will reinforce that this promise of being "clothed with the Holy Spirit" is for all Christians, and is essential to our being able to serve as Jesus' witnesses. In the chapter entitled "When Our Candle Becomes a Torch" we will illustrate this dynamic.

Chapter 7: The Spirit Empowered Samson

The Book of Judges records three occasions where the Spirit came "upon" Samson.

1. Judges 14:6

Samson walked about 20 miles west of his home in Jerusalem toward the Judean town of Timnah (Judges 14:1) – which at that time was occupied by the Philistines – in order to marry a daughter of the Philistines, a practice forbidden by Mosaic Law (Deuteronomy 7:3-4). On the way a young lion came roaring toward him (Judges 14:5).

> *Then the Spirit of the Lord rushed upon him, and although he had nothing in his hand, he tore the lion in pieces as one tears a young goat.* Judges 14:6, ESV

The same verse in other translations reads as follows:

- *The Spirit of the Lord came powerfully upon him,* (NIV).
- *The Spirit of the Lord came upon him mightily,* (NAS).

When the Spirit rushed "upon" him, the Spirit empowered
Samson to do a mighty work – to destroy a roaring lion with
his bare hands.

In a comparatively small way, I experienced the Holy Spirit
"rush" upon me, compelling me to step out of my comfort zone
and act. I was sitting in the audience at a Dunamis event as one
of my beloved mentors, Jon DeBruyn, who has since gone
home to glory, was teaching. As we neared the conclusion of
that session, the Holy Spirit suddenly "rushed upon" me, and
downloaded a clear understanding of what we as a group were
to do next. In a manner uncharacteristic of me, I sprang to my
feet, went to Jon, and shared the guidance that I had received.
He handed the microphone to me and invited me to implement
the plan – a plan that included us as a group gathering around
Tom and praying for him. The time of prayer for Tom proved
to be especially significant. When we finished praying, I
studied Tom's face and he looked deeply refreshed like a heavy
weight had been lifted from his shoulders.

2. Judges 14:19

After Samson caved-in to his Philistine wife's relentless
pleading for the answer to his riddle (Judges 14:12-14), she
betrayed him and relayed his answer to the Philistines. That
made Samson really angry. Scripture tells us:

> *The Spirit of the Lord rushed upon him [Samson], and
> he went down to Ashkelon and struck down thirty men
> of the town and took their spoil and gave the garments
> to those who had told the riddle. In hot anger he went
> back to his father's house.* Judges 14:19, ESV

The NAS translates it this way: *Then the Spirit of the Lord
came upon him mightily.*

Scripture does not say that the Spirit entered "into" Samson to transform his character but that the Spirit rushed "upon" him and empowered him to destroy thirty Philistines.[14]

3. Judges 15:14-15

Following an altercation with the family and friends of his Philistine wife from Timnah, Samson's own countrymen from Judah bound him with two new ropes and, in an effort to restore peace with the Philistines, brought Samson to them.

> *When he [Samson] came to Lehi, the Philistines came shouting to meet him. Then the Spirit of the Lord* rushed upon *him, and the ropes that were on his arms became as flax that has caught fire, and his bonds melted off his hands. And he found a fresh jawbone of a donkey, and put out his hand and took it, and with it he struck 1,000 men.* Judges 15:14-15, ESV

Once again the NAS translates the key phrase, *And the Spirit of the Lord* came upon him mightily.

No one can slaughter 1000 Philistines with the jawbone of a donkey unless he is empowered by the Spirit of God! Clearly credit goes to the Spirit for equipping Sampson to do this mighty work. The very next chapter in the Book of Judges

---

[14] The New Testament includes at least two examples of the Holy Spirit "rushing upon" someone:

    a) The Day of Pentecost in Acts 2:2, *And suddenly there came from heaven a sound like a mighty rushing wind, and it filled the entire house where they were sitting.* (ESV)

    b) In the confrontation between Peter and Simon the Magician in Acts 8:18-24, the Spirit apparently rushed upon Peter and a strong rebuke exploded from Peter's lips.

reveals how limited Samson was in his own strength. Delilah said:

> *"The Philistines are upon you, Samson!" And he*
> *awoke from his sleep and said, "I will go out as at*
> *other times and shake myself free." But he did not*
> *know that <u>the Lord had left him</u>. And the Philistines*
> *seized him and gouged out his eyes and brought him*
> *down to Gaza and bound him with bronze shackles.*
> *And he ground at the mill in the prison.*
> Judges 16:20-21, ESV

LESSONS LEARNED FROM SAMSON'S LIFE REGARDING EMPOWERMENT

From Samson's life we learn two timeless lessons regarding the empowering work of the Spirit.

1. The Spirit's work of empowerment is episodic.

The Spirit did not rush "upon" Sampson and "remain" "on" him. Rather, the Spirit remained on Samson only for as long as there was Divine work to accomplish. Then, the Spirit lifted.

As our study of the Spirit's work of empowerment unfolds we will see several more examples of the episodic nature of the Spirit's visitations. Like the touch-and-go landings of a pilot learning to fly, the Spirit touches down ... and then, when God's work is done, He lifts. This pattern also holds true in our day.

2. Empowerment does not necessarily result in character transformation.

The Spirit's empowering work in Samson's life did not change his core character. In many ways he remained impetuous and immature throughout his life. If I had a daughter I would not want her to date him.

Likewise, in our day – for reasons that we cannot explain – God occasionally empowers scoundrels to do remarkable works and speak amazing words. Michele Perry observed, "'Gifts can take you where your character can't keep you.' Gifts are given, but character is cultivated."[15] Although the ideal is to be both holy and empowered, sometimes – as in the case of Samson – God works miracles and brings conversions though people who have deep character defects.

Comparison:

- The inward work of the Holy Spirit produces character transformation in us.

- His outward work is the result of empowerment. The Holy Spirit flows out from us to benefit others.

Jesus' desire is that we grow in both areas.

---

[15] Michele Perry, "Supernatural Myth-Busters," (*Charisma Magazine*, 2013), 61.

Chapter 8: The Spirit Empowered Saul

The roots of the New Testament concept of "baptism with the Holy Spirit" (empowerment) reach deep into the soil of the Old Testament and include King Saul, Israel's first king. Saul was the king who, in a fit of rage, hurled a spear at David. David escaped but Saul relentlessly pursued him in an effort to kill him in order to secure the kingdom for his own son, Jonathan.

Prior to Saul's craziness, Scripture records two instances where the Spirit of the Lord rushed "upon" Saul impacting first His words, and second, his works.

The Spirit Rushed Upon Saul, Impacting His Words

Samuel spoke prophetically to Saul and said:

> *Then the Spirit of the Lord will <u>rush upon</u> you, and you will prophesy with them and be turned into another man.* 1 Samuel 10:6, ESV

What Samuel predicted came to pass.

> *When he [Saul] turned his back to leave Samuel, God gave him another heart. And all these signs came to pass that day. When they came to Gibeah, behold, a*

*group of prophets met him, and the Spirit of God
rushed upon him, and he prophesied among them.*
1 Samuel 10:9-10, ESV

Normally in the Old Testament, "prophecy" refers either to
fore-telling (i.e., predicting the future) or to forth-telling (i.e.,
proclaiming a message from the Lord). However, according to
the Reformation Study Bible, the "prophesying in view here
seems to be praising God and exhorting the people with
musical accompaniment."[16] Parallel examples where
"prophecy" means an outburst of praise and worship occur in 1
Chronicles 25:1-3 and Luke 1:67-77.

The big point I am making is this: When the Spirit rushed upon
him, King Saul opened his mouth and words streamed out – in
this case, prophetic words of praise. Saul's outburst was so
uncharacteristic of him and so surprising that the people who
witnessed his behavior coined a proverb, *Is Saul also among
the prophets?* (1 Samuel 10:12, ESV)[17]

Personally, I can identify with Saul. During the days that
followed my initial request for Jesus to baptize me with the
Holy Spirit, praise and worship streamed out of my heart – at
times, almost exploded out! – confirming to me that Jesus had,
in fact, answered my prayer. In a future chapter, I will tell this
story in more detail.

In the next verse (1 Samuel 10:13) we see a reminder of the
episodic nature of the Spirit's empowerment. By "episodic" I
mean that the Spirit's empowerment comes and goes. The

---

[16] *Reformation Study Bible,* R.C. Sproul, General Editor, (Orlando, FL:
Ligonier Ministries, 2005), 391.
[17] Additional examples where the Spirit's empowerment produced dynamic
words include Balaam (Numbers 24:2), and Jahaziel (2 Chronicles 20:14-
15).

Spirit "falls" and, once His work is done, He "lifts." Samuel recorded that,

> *When he [Saul] had finished prophesying, he came to the high place,* 1 Samuel 10:13, ESV.

The word "finished" implies that Saul's prophetic utterances had a starting point but they did not last forever. Eventually he "finished" prophesying.

In most cases in the Old Testament, in the New Testament, in the Book of Acts, and in our day, the Spirit's "empowerment" is episodic. When God's work in a person or situation has been accomplished, the Spirit "lifts:" the oil stops flowing (see 2 Kings 4:6). In time, however, we will see two exceptions to this rule: David (1 Samuel 16:13), and the Messiah.

The Spirit Rushed Upon Saul, Impacting His Works

In the narrative in 1 Samuel 11, Nahash the Ammonite came against Jabesh-Gilead and, in exchange for a peace treaty, demanded to gouge out the right eye of every man in that area (1 Samuel 11:2). Nahash's demand created a national crisis which, in turn, became the occasion for Saul's second experience of the Spirit's empowerment. We read in 1 Samuel 11:6, *The Spirit of God rushed upon Saul (*ESV).

Prior to the Spirit rushing upon him, Saul functioned as a reluctant leader who suffered from a bad case of low self-esteem.

> *Am I not a Benjamite, from the smallest tribe of Israel, and is not my clan the least of all the clans of the tribe of Benjamin? Why do you say such a thing to me?* 1 Samuel 9:21, NIV

> *Saul the son of Kish was taken by lot. But when they sought him, he could not be found. So they inquired again of the Lord, "Is there a man still to come?" and the Lord said, "Behold, he has <u>hidden</u> himself among the baggage."* 1 Samuel 10:21-22, ESV

After the Spirit rushed upon reluctant Saul, he demonstrated confident leadership.

> *Now, behold, Saul was coming from the field behind the oxen. And Saul said, "What is wrong with the people, that they are weeping?" So they told him the news of the men of Jabesh. And <u>the Spirit of God rushed upon Saul</u> when he heard these words, and his anger was greatly kindled. He took a yoke of oxen and cut them in pieces and sent them throughout all the territory of Israel by the hand of the messengers, saying, "Whoever does not come out after Saul and Samuel, so shall it be done to his oxen!" Then the dread of the Lord fell upon the people, and they came out as one man.* 1 Sam. 11:5-7, ESV

The Spirit's empowerment transformed Saul from a hesitant leader to a confident general. He responded quickly, decisively, and courageously to a national crisis, mustered an army, and saved Jabesh-Gilead.

Relevance

The result of the Spirit's empowerment in Saul's life establishes a pattern for the Spirit's empowerment in the New Testament, in the Book of Acts, and in our day. For example, in the Book of Acts, the Holy Spirit came "upon" those gathered in the upper room, impacting their words and works.

- Words: They spoke in tongues (Acts 2:4), and Peter preached powerfully (Acts 2:14-42).

- Works: In the name of Jesus, Peter and John healed a crippled beggar (Acts 3:1-10).

You can count on this: When the Holy Spirit falls on ordinary people in our day, in His perfect time and in His creative way He will impact their words and/or their works. For example, I watched and listened as the Holy Spirit fell upon a young professional at a Dunamis Conference. He fell to his knees, lifted his hands in praise, and burst forth in tongues.

Chapter 9: The Spirit Empowered Amasai

Imagine for a moment that you are part of a small group that
met to discuss a very important issue. You talk, debate, pray,
and talk some more ... but you are at an impasse. The options
and alternatives are clear but you do not know which to choose.
Then, quietly ... yet dynamically the Spirit of the Lord falls
upon one of the people seated at the table and she began to
speak. As you listen you hear intensity, clarity, and truth. You
sense that God is speaking to the group through her and telling
you the step-of-faith that you are to take.

The Old Testament books of 1 and 2 Chronicles record four
instances where the Spirit of the Lord came "upon" a person
and subsequently empowered that person to speak a word from
the Lord to those who were present.[18] Amasai (Am-a-sai) is a
classic example of this dynamic.

Join with me in using a little sanctified imagination to re-live a
tense moment in David's life when he was on the run from
Saul.

One afternoon, David was standing on top of a hill named
Ziklag when he spotted in the distance a band of 30 men
approaching his camp. David sent out a few scouts and they

---

[18] 1 Chronicles 12:17-18; 2 Chronicles 15:1-2; 20:14-15; 24:20

reported back that the men were from the tribes Benjamin and Judah. Intuitively David's guard went up. Why? Because King Saul was from the Tribe of Benjamin and Saul was trying to kill him. "Maybe," thought David, "these men have been sent by Saul to assassinate me. Maybe they are pretending to be friendly when, in fact, their real intent is to use deception to get close enough to me to kill me. But, on the other hand, maybe they have had enough of Saul's craziness. Perhaps their sincere intent is to pledge loyalty to me and my men."

I do not believe that David knew which perspective was true when he went out to meet them. David said,

> *If you come peacefully to me to help me, my heart shall be united with you; but if to betray me to my adversaries, since there is no wrong in my hands, may the God of our fathers look on it and decide.*
> 1 Chronicles 12:17, NIV

Imagine …

- Behind David stood 200 skilled warriors who were loyal to him.
- In front of David stood 30 newcomers. Were they friends or foes?

David made an opening statement (12:17).

Then, silence.

Every one present kept his guard up. Their hands rested on their bows, slings, swords, and spears as the two groups studied one another. How will David know what to do next?

The silence seemed to last forever.

At that critical moment, God intervened.

> *Then the Spirit <u>clothed</u> Amasai, chief of the thirty, and
> he said, "We are yours, O David, and with you, O son
> of Jesse! Peace, peace to you, and peace to your
> helpers! For your God helps you."*
> 1 Chronicles 12:18, ESV

Amasai stopped speaking … and once again, a tense silence.

The standoff continued as David weighed what he had just
heard. He cast a quick glance at the men behind him … and the
men in front of him. I imagine that David was thinking to
himself: "Can I trust these guys? They are skilled warriors
from Saul's tribe. They could do a lot of damage in a short time
if they turn against us." Yet, deep within his spirit David knew
that Amasai's words were not part of a carefully rehearsed
speech; rather, they were an unplanned outburst that carried a
ring of sincerity.

David had a choice:

- To step out in faith, believe the words, and welcome the
  men.
- To shrink back in fear, doubt the words, and send the
  men away.

David took a deep breath … and chose the response of faith.
Scripture tells us:

> *Then David received them and made them officers of
> his troops.* 1 Chronicles 12:18, ESV

I wonder …

Do you think that Amasai was surprised when he heard those words coming out of his mouth?

Have you ever been in a situation where you heard yourself saying things that you did not plan to say? And when you spoke, you spoke with a clarity, conviction, and energy that surprised even you? If yes, then you have experienced an "Amasai moment."

Several years ago, I attended a Dunamis Fellowship Conference in Black Mountain, North Carolina. On the schedule for our final evening was a time for prayer ministry and anointing with oil for empowerment. During a brief break just before the meeting, our leader, Brad Long, mentioned that he thought he would sit on sidelines and watch as prayer teams ministered to participants who were seeking a fresh infilling with the Holy Spirit. Immediately I had a strong sense that Brad was not to do that. I looked straight at him and before I know what was happening, I heard myself saying with clarity and intensity: "No, Brad, you are to lay hands on people and pray for them." The force of that statement caught both of us by surprise. John Chang, who was standing next to me, looked at me, looked at Brad, and then affirmed, "Yes Brad, I believe that you are to lay hands on people tonight and pray for them." Brad did … and it was glorious!

I imagine that when Amasai laid his head on his pillow that night and thought back through the events of the day, he felt both humbled and thrilled to know that God had chosen to come upon him, to speak through him, and to advance His purposes for Israel.

I expect that prior to this moment, most of us never, ever, heard of Amasai. I hope that as a result of this study, we will not only know who he is but also be open to – even desire – to be used by God as he was. I sincerely long for my life, and our lives, to be filled with "Amasai moments."

A Summary of the Spirit's Work in the Lives of Gideon, Samson, Saul, and Amasai

	Text	Termin-ology	Result: Dynamic Action!	Lesson Learned Re: Empowerment
Gideon	Judges 6:34	*Spirit clothed* (ESV)	His "candle" became a "torch," and he led 300 soldiers to defeat 135,000 Midianites.	The Spirit can transform timid men into mighty warriors.
Samson	Judges 14:6, 19; 15:14-15; (16:28, implied)	*Spirit rushed upon* (ESV)	Tore apart a young lion. Slaughtered 30, then 1000, Philistines.	The Spirit's work of empowerment: 1) is episodic and 2) does not necessarily result in character transformation.

King Saul	1 Samuel 10:6, 9-13; 11:1ff	*Spirit rushed upon* (ESV)	Saul prophesied. Saul defeated the Ammonites.	The Spirit may propel us: 1) to speak powerful words and/or 2) to do mighty works. Also, we see once again the episodic nature of empowerment, 1 Samuel 10:13.
Amasai	1 Chronicles 12:18	*Spirit clothed* (ESV)	Amasai spoke with passion and authority.	The Spirit's timing is "spot-on" (just right).

Chapter 10: The Spirit Empowered David

We turn now to consider an exception to the rule. Generally, the Holy Spirit's work of empowerment is episodic. However, in the case of David and David's greater Son, the Messiah, the Spirit "rested upon" them.

Following God's rejection of King Saul, the Lord sent the Prophet Samuel to Bethlehem to anoint a new king. After seven of his sons passed in front of Samuel, Samuel asked Jesse if he had more. In response, Jesse summoned David from the field, and the Lord said:

> *"Arise, anoint him, for this is he." Then Samuel took the horn of oil and anointed him in the midst of his brothers. And the Spirit of the Lord <u>rushed upon</u> David <u>from that day forward</u>. And Samuel rose up and went to Ramah.* 1 Samuel 16:12-13, ESV[19]

In earlier studies the same phrase (rushed upon) was used to describe the Spirit's action

- in Samson's life. Judges 14:6,19; 15:14, and

---

[19] Compare the NIV: *So Samuel took the horn of oil and anointed him in the presence of his brothers, and <u>from that day on</u> the Spirit of the LORD came upon David in power.* I Samuel 16:13

- in Saul's life. 1 Samuel 10:10; 11:6. Cf. Numbers 11:25

Clearly, when we read that the Spirit of the Lord *rushed upon David* (1 Samuel 16:13), we are reading the language of empowerment. The Spirit of the Lord manifested His empowering presence in and through David's words and works.

1. David's words

Example: *The Spirit of the LORD spoke through me; his word was on my tongue,* 2 Samuel 23:2, NIV. Empowered by the Spirit, David wrote scores of anointed Psalms.

2. David's works

Example: *Saul has slain his thousands, and David his tens of thousands,* 1 Samuel 18:7, NIV.

In our studies up to this point, we noted the episodic nature of the Spirit's work of empowerment. Once the job God wanted done was finished, the Spirit lifted. In contrast, the Spirit's work of empowerment in David's life was permanent: it had a starting point but no ending point.[20]

Why did David receive and experience life-long empowerment?

---

[20]At some level David was aware that he was being helped by the Holy Spirit and that he [David] was not in control of the Spirit. Following his affair with Bathsheba, David wrote: *Do not cast me from your presence or take your Holy Spirit from me,* Psalm 51:11, NIV. On another occasion David cried out, *Teach me to do your will, for you are my God; may your good Spirit lead me on level ground.* Psalm 143:10, NIV

Option A: Is Scripture signaling a change, a new trend, a new pattern, or a new mode of the Spirit's operation? Are we to expect that, from that time forward, throughout the New Testament, and into our day, the episodic nature of the Spirit's work of empowerment will cease, and that He will permanently rest upon people? Or,

Option B: Is Scripture drawing our attention to David's unique role in Biblical history?

The answer is "B." David is unique in that he is a prototype of Christ.

David, a Prototype of Christ

We are familiar with the concept of prototypes in fields such as the automotive industry. Engineers design and build a prototype car; and in time, they unveil the finished product. In a similar way, David functioned as a prototype of Jesus Christ. He prefigured his greater Son, Jesus.[21]

Just as the Spirit remained on David, so He will rest upon the Messiah. The great Prophet Isaiah declared,

> *There shall come forth a shoot from the stump of Jesse,*
> *   and a branch from his roots shall bear fruit.*
> *And the Spirit of the Lord shall <u>rest upon</u> him,*
> *   the Spirit of wisdom and understanding,*
> *   the Spirit of counsel and might,*
> *   the Spirit of knowledge and the fear of the Lord.*
> Isaiah 11:1-2, ESV. See also Isaiah 42:1; 61:1

---

[21] David was not like Jesus in all ways. E.g., David sinned but Jesus remained righteous.

Strong's Concordance (#05117) defines the verb "rest" as: "to rest; to settle down and remain."

The Spirit's empowerment in David's life and in Jesus' was permanent. However, for us, the Spirit's empowering presence continues to be episodic. In other words, the Spirit remains "upon" us as long as there is divine work to do; and, once the task is finished, the Spirit lifts. The oil stops flowing.

Postscript

After reading this chapter, a friend wrote to me, "The statement about the Spirit being episodic (not permanent) in the lives of New Testament Christians is contrary to my understanding of how He operates. I understand that the Holy Spirit was episodic in the Old Testament but that He is always present with believers in the New Testament. Here are some scriptures supporting that position:

- *I will ask the Father, and he will give you another Helper, to be with you forever.* John 14:16-17, ESV

- *You, however, are not in the flesh but in the Spirit, if in fact the Spirit of God dwells in you. Anyone who does not have the Spirit of Christ does not belong to him.* Romans 8:9, ESV

I responded by saying, "Yes, you are correct: the Holy Spirit dwells permanently "in" New Testament Christians. However, a close study of the New Testament requires us to make a distinction between the Holy Spirit's works of transformation (sanctification) and empowerment. He dwells permanently in us (as you noted in John 14 and Romans 8) in order to do a variety of things including produce Christ-like character qualities (spiritual fruit). In addition, on occasion He comes "upon" us to empower us to advance the Father's agenda by equipping us to do mighty works and/or speak dynamic words. The Spirit's empowering work in the lives of New Testament Christians continues to be episodic."

Chapter 11: Looking Ahead

EMPOWERMENT AVAILABLE FOR ALL

On at least two occasions, God prompted Old Testament leaders to peer into the future and declare that the day will come when God will empower not only a few, select leaders; but also scores of ordinary people.

Moses, Numbers 11

After the Spirit fell on the seventy elders in Numbers 11, Joshua (Moses' trusted assistant) observed that the Spirit also fell upon two men – Eldad and Medad – who had remained in the camp. When the Spirit fell upon them, they, too, prophesied. Alarmed, Joshua blurted out:

> *"My lord Moses, stop them." But Moses said to him, "Are you jealous for my sake? Would that all the Lord's people were prophets, that the Lord would put his Spirit on them!"* Numbers 11:28-30, ESV

Joel 2:28-29

Following the exile (586 B.C.), God spoke a message of hope through the Prophet Joel.

> *And it shall come to pass afterward,*
> *   that I will pour out my Spirit on <u>all</u> flesh;*
> *your sons and your daughters shall prophesy,*
> *   your old men shall dream dreams,*
> *   and your young men shall see visions.*
> *29 Even on the male and female servants*
> *   in those days I will pour out my Spirit.*
>   Joel 2:28-29, ESV

Joel's choice of words aligns with the vocabulary of empowerment that we saw in the lives of Gideon, Samson, Saul, Amasai, and David. The unique feature in Joel is this: Whereas the Spirit's work of empowerment in the Old Testament was limited to a few, select prophets, priests, kings, and judges, Joel foresaw a day when empowerment will extend to ordinary people – men and women, slaves and free, young and old.

On the Day of Pentecost (Acts 2), God fulfilled Joel's prophecy: God poured out His Spirit upon all the people who were in that place. It is not by accident that Dr. Luke recorded that the immediate outgrowth of Pentecost was powerful words (the Spirit empowered Peter to preach, Acts 2:14ff.), and might works (the Spirit empowered Peter to heal a lame man, Acts 3:1-10).

The Prophets Isaiah and Ezekiel also anticipated future empowerment.

*I will pour water on the thirsty land, and streams on the
dry ground; I will pour my Spirit upon your
offspring, and my blessing on your descendants.*
Isaiah 44:3, ESV

*And I will not hide my face anymore from them, when I
pour out my Spirit upon the house of Israel, declares
the Lord God.* Ezekiel 39:29, ESV

An "Ah-ha" Moment

In the year 2000, a major shift occurred in my mind and heart
when I initially realized the link between the word "upon" in
Acts 1:8 (*"But you will receive power when the Holy Spirit has
come upon you,"* ESV) and the pattern of empowerment in the
Old Testament. Suddenly I realized that Jesus' choice of words
was not random; rather, Jesus reached back into the Old
Testament and carefully selecting a word that described the
pattern of empowerment that had occurred in days of old. In
the context of Acts 1:8, Jesus promised that the same Holy
Spirit who empowered Old Testament saints was about to
empower His disciples, equipping them to advance the gospel
with greater effectiveness.

My initial response to this insight was one of anger. I had been
reared in a Christian home, attended a Christian college, and
earned a master's degree in divinity from a respected seminary.
Yet, no one had schooled me in the empowering dimension of
the Holy Spirit's work.

My second response was one of sadness. For years I had
labored long and hard in various ministries seeing limited
spiritual fruit result. I wondered how much more there could
have been if only I had been introduced earlier in my Christian
life to this aspect of the Holy Spirit's work.

As the Holy Spirit enlightened my understanding, I began to hunger and thirst for His empowering presence in my life. In a future chapter I will describe my baptism with the Holy Spirit.

THE HOLY SPIRIT'S <u>INWARD WORK</u> ANTICIPATED

Before we leave the Old Testament we must pause to note that the prophets foresaw a day when the Spirit would not only come "upon" people to empower them but also dwell "in" them to transform them from the inside out.

The Prophet Ezekiel anticipated the Holy Spirit's inward work when he wrote,

> *I will give you a new heart, and a new spirit I will put within you. And I will remove the heart of stone from your flesh and give you a heart of flesh. And I will put my Spirit <u>within</u> you, and cause you to walk in my statutes and be careful to obey my rules.*
> Ezekiel 36:26-27, ESV. Cf. Ezekiel 11:19-20

A heart of stone is a heart that is unable to respond to God with love and obedience. Remember, there are very few references, if any, in the Old Testament to the Spirit living <u>in</u> people. However, Ezekiel foresaw a change. In the future God's Spirit will also dwell within people, transforming them from the inside-out into loving and obedient children of God whose lives display the fruit of the Spirit (Galatians 5:22-23).[22]

---

[22] In a similar light, when the Prophet Jeremiah (31:33) spoke of the New Covenant, he declared that God will put His Law <u>within</u> His people.

Relevance

In some circles in our day an emphasis is placed on the Spirit's inward work of transformation, and in others, on His outward work[23] of empowerment. Either-or is not good enough: as New Testament Christians we are called to know the Holy Spirit in fullness. By comparison, if I know my spouse's personality and skills as a wife and mother but have no concept of her strengths in her career, I do not know her in fullness. Likewise, if we know the Spirit's inward work but not His empowering work, we only know Him in part.

- The Holy Spirit lives within us to transform us into Christ's likeness; and,

- He comes upon us to empower us to advance Jesus' agenda.

Let us resolve, with God's help, to live and serve in the fullness of the Spirit!

Where to Start

A few months ago I received the following note from a lady who was in the beginning stages of learning about the empowering dimension of the Holy Spirit's work, in which she revealed a heart that God will honor.

> Hello Pastor Phil, I'm glad you're preaching about the Holy Spirit as many Christians do not readily understand how the Spirit helps us. I asked the Holy Spirit to bring me underneath His mantel in February.

---

[23] "Outward" in the sense that the Holy Spirit flows out from us to benefit others.

In other words I asked to be baptized in the Spirit.
Believe me, His presence is known by me. I have found
myself brought to repentance for many things that have
grieved the Lord. Indeed, the Spirit convicts of sin.
And, He gives assurance of forgiveness. Blessing.

For Further Reflection

Chapters 6-11: The Spirit Empowered Gideon, Samson, Saul, Amasai, and David

1. In your own words summarize one of the main points in
   the chapters pertaining to the Spirit's work in the Old
   Testament.

2. Talk about one of the first times when you heard a
   teacher distinguish between the Holy Spirit "within"
   and the Holy Spirit "upon."

3. In which of your current relationships or circumstances
   would it be helpful to experience an additional measure
   of spiritual authority and power? What might happen
   when the Spirit rushes upon you?!?

PART IV: THE HOLY SPIRIT IN THE NEW TESTAMENT

In the chapters that follow, we will focus on the empowering dimension of the Holy Spirit's work in the New Testament including its relevance for us in our day.

Chapter 12: Jesus, A Spirit-Empowered Man

This chapter addresses an issue that has been a stumbling block to many people who are seeking to understand and experience empowerment. For years I did not hold this view. However, I have come to understand that while on earth, Jesus Christ functioned as a Holy Spirit empowered man.

The Prophet Isaiah declared that the Messiah will minister as God's servant to bring both justice and light to the nations (Isaiah 42:1-4), opening blind eyes and releasing prisoners from darkness (Isaiah 42:6-7). The Messiah will also preach good news to the poor, bind up the brokenhearted, set captives free, and proclaim the year of the Lord's favor (Isaiah 61:1f).

The New Testament reveals that Jesus, the Messiah, fulfilled these prophecies.

How did Jesus accomplish His mission and ministry?

Options:

1. Jesus was God. Of course, as God, He had the authority and power to do anything He wanted done.

2. While on earth, Jesus functioned as a Holy Spirit empowered man.

Prior to the year 2000, if you had asked me, "Why was Jesus able to perform miracles?" I would have answered, "Because He was God. But I am not God. Therefore, do not expect me to heal the sick or drive out demons." One author summarized my perspective when he wrote, "Many Christians have attributed Jesus' power and miracles to His divine nature. … This orientation, however, really implies a quantum difference between Jesus and us. He is God. We are only human beings."[24]

Factors That Changed My Thinking

While attending a Dunamis Fellowship event in North Carolina in 2000, my roommate, Tom, prodded me to take another look at Philippians 2:7, and answer the question, "Of what did Jesus empty Himself?"

Regarding Jesus, Paul wrote in Philippians 2:

---

[24] Zeb Bradford Long and Douglas McMurry, *Gateways to Empowered Ministry* (The Dunamis Project, PRMI.org, Revised 2006), 186.

... who, though he was in the form of God, did not count equality with God a thing to be grasped, but <u>emptied himself,</u> by taking the form of a servant ...   Philippians 2:6-8, ESV

Emptied Himself

Scholars have poured gallons of ink into an effort to explain what Paul did and did not mean in Philippians 2:7. Here are a few of their comments each of which I agree with:

- The ESV Study Bible states that "The 'emptying' consisted of his becoming human, not of his giving up any part of His true deity."[25]

- Dr. John Walvoord observed, "Christ did not empty Himself of deity, but of its outward manifestation. He emptied Himself by taking the form of a servant. ... The incarnation did not change the person and attributes of Christ in His divine nature, but added to it a complete human nature. ... Christ voluntarily, moment by moment, submitted to human limitations apart from sin.[26]

- Another scholar wrote, "Conservative theologians interpret this passage to mean that Jesus took on the limitations of humanity. This involved a veiling of His preincarnate glory (John 17:5) and the voluntary non-use of some of His divine prerogatives during the time He was on earth (Matthew 24:36)."[27]

---

[25] *English Standard Version Study Bible*, (Wheaton, IL: Crossway Bible, 2008), 2283.
[26] John Walvoord, "Philippians 2: At The Name Of Jesus Every Knee Should Bow," http://preceptaustin.org/philippians_25-11.htm#2:7
[27] http://preceptaustin.org/philippians_25-11.htm#2:7

Evangelical Christians affirm that Jesus was (and is) truly God and truly man. Jesus did not stop being God during His time on earth; however, He did empty Himself of something – apparently of His divine prerogatives. Jesus added a human nature to His divine nature and lived as a man among men except that He never sinned. In support of this understanding the author of Hebrews wrote,

> *Therefore he had to be made like his brothers in every respect.* Hebrews 2:17, ESV

> *For we do not have a high priest who is unable to sympathize with our weaknesses, but one who in every respect has been tempted as we are, yet without sin.* Hebrews 4:15, ESV

A Man among Men, Empowered by the Holy Spirit

In light of the above observations, I have come to embrace the view held by the following scholars:

- Sermon by R.C. Sproul: "Jesus has the divine nature from the moment of His conception all the way till now and on to eternity. So what is the significance of the Holy Spirit coming upon Him? It is the Holy Spirit anointing the human nature of Jesus. We tend to think that the miracles that Jesus performed He performed in His divine nature. No! He performed them in His human nature through the power of the Holy Spirit that was given to Him at His baptism. Here [at His baptism] is where God is empowering Jesus to fulfill the mission that He has."[28]

---

[28] R.C. Sproul, sermon: "Baptism & Temptation of Jesus." Ligonier

- Talbot Theology professor J.P. Moreland: "When I was saved in the late 1960s, I was taught that Jesus' miracles proved he was God because he did them from His divine nature. It has become clear to me, however, that this was wrong, for Jesus' public ministry was done as He, a perfect man, did what he saw his Father doing in dependence on the filling of the Holy Spirit."[29]

- Dallas Seminary professor Dr. Thomas Constable: "Luke viewed the power of God as extrinsic[30] to Jesus (cf. John 5:1-19). Jesus did not perform miracles out of His divine nature. He laid those powers aside at the Incarnation. Rather, He did His miracles in the power of God's Spirit—who was on Him and in Him—as a prophet. ... In Acts, Luke would stress that the same Spirit is on and in every believer today, and He is the source of our power as He was the source of Jesus' power."[31]

- R.C. Sproul: "The idea that Jesus' two natures were like alternating electrical circuits, so that sometimes He acted in His humanity and sometimes in His Divinity, is also mistaken."[32]

When He sent Jesus to earth, the Father leveled the playing field. Jesus added a human nature to His divine nature and

---

Ministries: Message of the Month, February 2014.

[29] J.P. Moreland, *Kingdom Triangle* (Grand Rapids, MI: Zondervan, 2007), 174.

[30] Extrinsic: Not part of the essential nature of someone or something; coming or operating from outside. Merriam-Webster Dictionary online.

[31] Dr. Thomas Constable, in his Commentary on Luke 5:17. We will point out that the Spirit is not automatically "on" every believer.

[32] *Reformation Study Bible,* R.C. Sproul, General Editor, (Orlando, FL: Ligonier Ministries, 2005), 1836.

voluntarily limited Himself to function on earth as a man among men – yes, a remarkable man – nevertheless, a man. Jesus voluntarily laid aside His ability to operate out of His divine side. He chose to live His life on earth as a human being.

Jesus' Baptism: A Turning Point
Matthew 3:13-17; Mark 1:9-11; Luke 3:21-22; John 1:29-34

Prior to His baptism, there is no record of Jesus teaching,[33] preaching, performing miracles or casting out evil spirits. Based on the gospel's record, however, we can say with confidence that following His baptism in water and with the Holy Spirit, a major shift occurred. The Holy Spirit descended upon Him (Luke 3:21-22), and He went forth in the power of the Spirit (Luke 4:14) to preach, teach, and do miracles.

In a similar way, a significant shift occurs in our lives when we ask Jesus to baptize us with the Holy Spirit. Prior to that point the Holy Spirit's primary work occurs "in" us, transforming us little by little into Christ-like servants. A turning point occurs in our lives when we humbly, sincerely, and in faith ask Jesus to baptize us with the Holy Spirit. He does.

Prior to our baptism with the Spirit, we exercised some of the functional gifts of the Spirit (Romans 12:1-8) and saw much fruit from abiding in Christ (John 15:1-17). After our baptism with the Spirit, Jesus adds to our functional gifts *the manifestations of the Spirit for the common good* (1 Corinthians 12:7), and we are equipped, as Jesus was, to go forth in the Holy Spirit's power (Luke 4:14) to preach, teach, disciple, prophesy, speak words of wisdom and knowledge, heal the sick, and drive out evil spirits.

---

[33]Minor exception: Jesus, age 12, Luke 2:41-50.

In a few chapters we will refine this analogy in order to better define and describe what happens when we are "baptized with the Holy Spirit."

Jesus' Understanding of the Source of His Power

> *But if it is by the Spirit of God that I cast out demons, then the Kingdom of God has come upon you.* Mt. 12:28, ESV

> *The Spirit of the Lord is upon me.* Luke 4:18, ESV

In these statements, Jesus Himself declared that He was functioning as a Spirit-empowered man (Luke 4:14; Philippians 2:7). He did not cast out demons by His divine nature, or by Beelzebub's power, but by the Spirit of God. While at Cornelius' house, the Apostle Peter expressed a similar perspective when he said, *God anointed Jesus of Nazareth with the Holy Spirit and with power. He went about doing good and healing all who were oppressed by the devil, for God was with him,* Acts 10:38, ESV. God was with Jesus in and through the Person of the Holy Spirit. The Holy Spirit empowered Jesus to teach, preach, and cast out demons.

Implication

There is hope for us! Through the power and authority of the same Holy Spirit who empowered Jesus, we too, in response to Jesus' guidance, may carry forward the ministries that He began. When empowered by the Holy Spirit, we, too, as ordinary men and women, may be used by Jesus to preach the word, heal the sick, and drive out evil spirits.

Reality Check

Do I go around doing these things? Honestly, for several years I have been on a major learning curve. A few months ago (2013) a lady approached me and explained that she had been struggling for several weeks with migraine headaches. I rested my hand on her head and prayed for her healing. A few weeks later she sent an email and reported that she has not had a migraine since the day we prayed. In June 2014, she sent a follow-up note saying, "Still no migraines, as a matter of fact no headaches at all, Praise God!" All glory to Jesus! He is the ultimate healer, not me.

If the Messiah Himself relied on the Holy Spirit's empowerment to accomplish His God-given mission and ministry, why do we tend to believe that we can get along just fine without it? If the Messiah needed the Spirit's empowerment, how much more do we! The truth is this: God gets His work done not by might, nor by power, but by His Spirit (Zechariah 4:6).

Chapter 13: Pentecost

As I noted in an earlier chapter, in a 2007 edition of Newsweek magazine, author and radio personality Garrison Keillor was asked to choose what he considered to be the five most important books ever written. Some readers were probably surprised to find that he ranked the Book of Acts at the top of his list. When describing it, Keillor offered this concise but potent summation: "The flames lit on their little heads and bravely and dangerously went they onward."

In the Old Testament, Pentecost occurred 50 days after the beginning of Passover. It was also known as "The Feast of Weeks," and "The Feast of Harvest." In the New Testament, Pentecost occurred 50 days after Christ's crucifixion.

Events Leading to Pentecost

1. Joel's Prophecy, Joel 2:28-29, ESV

> *And it shall come to pass afterward,*
> *that I will pour out my Spirit on all flesh;*
> *your sons and your daughters shall prophesy,*
> *your old men shall dream dreams,*
> *and your young men shall see visions.*
> *29 Even on the male and female servants*
> *in those days I will pour out my Spirit.*

Inspired by the Spirit, Joel declared that the empowering work of the Holy Spirit would expand beyond a few, select leaders and become available to all flesh – men, women, young, and old … potentially including you and me!

2. The Holy Spirit came to live <u>in</u> the Apostles, John 20:22

On the evening of the same day that God the Father raised Jesus from the dead, Jesus appeared to His Apostles[34] who were huddled together behind locked doors for fear of the Jews. When they recognized Jesus, they rejoiced. Then Jesus said to them:

> *"Peace be with you. As the Father has sent me, even so I am sending you." And when he had said this, he breathed on them and said to them, "<u>Receive the Holy Spirit</u>."* John 20:21-22, ESV

What happened? And, why does it matter?

Some commentators are not sure what to do with this text. For example,

- The footnote in the Reformation Study Bible reads, "This occasion is a foreshadowing of the fullness of the Spirit to be bestowed on the church at Pentecost."[35] In other words, nothing happened. Rather, the Apostles merely observed Jesus acting dramatically.

---

[34] Except Judas and Thomas, John 20:24.
[35] *Reformation Study Bible* (ESV), 2005, 1553.

- Hoskyns and Morris describe Jesus' words and actions as a preparatory event for Pentecost.[36]

- According to Vincent, this was a symbolic act patterned after some of the symbolic actions of the Old Testament prophets.[37]

- In the footnotes of Crossways' Study Bible we read, "When Jesus breathed on them and said, "Receive the Holy Spirit,' it is best understood as a foretaste of what would happen when the Holy Spirit was given at Pentecost."[38]

- Wayne Grudem agrees. This is "probably an acted-out prophecy of what would happen to them at Pentecost. … Therefore, His words are looking forward to what would happen at Pentecost."[39]

Are the above esteemed authorities correct? In the context of John's Gospel, what happened – if anything – when Jesus breathed on the Apostles and said, "*Receive the Holy Spirit*"?

"Receive" is one of John's favorite words. For example:

> But to all who did *receive* him, who believed in his name, he gave the right to become children of God.
> John 1:12, ESV

---

[36] Fritz Rienecker and Cleon Rogers, Jr., *Linguistic Key to the Greek New Testament* (Grand Rapids, MI: Zondervan, Regency Reference Library, 1980), 260.

[37] Vincent Word Studies online.

[38] *English Standard Version Study Bible*, (Wheaton, IL: Crossway Bible, 2008), 2070.

[39] Wayne Grudem, *Systematic Theology* (Grand Rapids, MI, 1994), 769.

On the last day of the feast, the great day, Jesus stood up and cried out, "If anyone thirsts, let him come to me and drink." ... Now this he said about the Spirit, whom those who believed in him were to <u>receive</u>, for as yet the Spirit had not been given, because Jesus was not yet glorified. John 7:37,39, ESV

Truly, truly, I say to you, whoever receives the one I send <u>receives</u> me, and whoever receives me receives the one who sent me. John 13:20, ESV

To receive Jesus is to open the door of our hearts and welcome Him in.[40] We agree with Hummel who noted that "an impartation actually took place."[41] In John 20:22, the verb "receive" is an imperative: it is a command. In every other situation, when Jesus issued a command, something happened. Why should we expect anything less here?

The opposite of "to receive" the Holy Spirit is to reject Him, to resist Him, to shut Him out. That is not what the Apostles did. They welcomed Him in, and the Holy Spirit came to dwell within them.

The point that John makes in John 20:22 is that the Apostles were converted on the day that Jesus breathed on them and said, "Receive the Holy Spirit." At that moment, they were born again. As Dennis Bennett observed, "The Holy Spirit came to live in them, bringing their spirits to life – they were born again of the Spirit."[42] This was their spiritual birthday.

---

[40] Cf. Galatians 3:1-2; Romans 8:13-16; 1 Thessalonians 4:8

[41] Charles Hummel, *Fire in the Fireplace* (Downers Grove, IL: InterVarsity Press, Second Edition 1979), 240-241.

[42] Dennis Bennett, *The Holy Spirit and You* (North Brunswick, NJ: Bridge-Logos Publishers, 1971), 26.

It is also fitting to link Jesus' action in John 20:22 to God's life-giving work in Genesis 2:

> *Then the Lord God formed man of dust from the ground, and breathed into his nostrils the breath of life; and man became a living being.* Genesis 2:7, NAS

Just as God's breath gave lifeless Adam both physical life and spiritual life, so Jesus' breath in John 20:22 imparted spiritual life to the Apostles.

What is the Significance of This for Us?

Notice the 40-day time lapse between the disciples' conversion (John 20:22), and Jesus' ascension (Acts 1:6-11). Following Jesus' ascension, the disciples obeyed Jesus' command to not depart from Jerusalem, but wait there ("tarry," Luke 24:49, KJV) until they were clothed with power from on high (Luke 24:49). Ten days later, Pentecost occurred (Acts 2:1-4). They were baptized with the Holy Spirit and empowered for more effective witness and service.

The point we must see is this: from Jesus' perspective, breathing the Holy Spirit into His disciples was good, but not good enough. Why? Because Jesus knew that the disciples needed something more in order to accomplish their humanly-impossible assignment of taking the gospel to the nations (Acts 1:8). They needed to experience Pentecost: they needed to be empowered by the Holy Spirit (Acts 2:1-4) in order to succeed. (So do we!) Hence, on the Day of Pentecost, Jesus sent the Holy Spirit upon them to equip them to accomplish their mission.

I recognize that the disciples' position in history, as recorded in the Book of Acts, was unique in that they bridged the old and new eras. Nevertheless, Jesus could have caused conversion and empowerment to occur on the same day just as He did for Cornelius (Acts 10:44-48). But He did not do so. Why not? Could it be that He was establishing a pattern for some of us to follow??

The implications for us are plain:

- Conversion is essential (the Holy Spirit coming to live within us).
- Empowerment is essential (the Holy Spirit coming upon to initiate us into power ministries).
- A time gap may occur between our conversion and our empowerment.

Pentecost: The Disciples' Baptism with the Holy Spirit

In Acts 2:1-4, Dr. Luke did not use the phrase "baptized with the Holy Spirit" to describe the events that occurred on the Day of Pentecost. However, Jesus' statements in Acts 1:4-8 make it clear that, on the Day of Pentecost, the disciples, who were obediently waiting and praying, were, in fact, baptized with the Holy Spirit.

> *And while staying with them he ordered them not to depart from Jerusalem, but to wait for the promise of the Father, which, he said, "you heard from me; for John baptized with water, but you will be <u>baptized with the Holy Spirit</u> not many days from now."*
> Acts 1:4-5, ESV

Jesus' words in these verses are also linked to John the Baptist's promise at the beginning of the gospels. John the Baptist declared:

I [John] baptize you with water for repentance, but he
who is coming after me is mightier than I, whose
sandals I am not worthy to carry. He will baptize
you with the Holy Spirit and fire. Matthew 3:11, ESV.
Parallels: Mark 1:7-8; Luke 3:13; John 1:32-33

The Holy Spirit's Three-step Movement

On the Day of Pentecost, the 120 who were gathered in the
Upper Room were clothed with power from on high (Luke
24:49; cf. Judges 6:34; 1 Chronicles 12:18).

The Holy Spirit moved
1. from above them,
2. to upon them,
3. to within them (Acts 2:1-4). The Holy Spirit clothed
   Himself with them.

He became their engine. This is their baptism with the Holy
Spirit. They were filled with the Holy Spirit ... and the rest is
history.

Why do we point out this progression?

Because, often this pattern repeats itself when the Holy Spirit
comes "upon" us, and we experience the empowering work of
the Holy Spirit.

Pentecost, A Hinge Event

Before the Day of Pentecost, the disciples huddled together in
an upper room and prayed.

After, they went out boldly and witnessed by word and deed to the resurrection of Jesus Christ.

Hinge Events: Review

	Before	After
Jesus' baptism with the Holy Spirit.	• Limited teaching, Luke 2:46-47 • No miracles • No casting out evil spirits	Jesus stepped out in the Spirit's power to resist temptation, teach, preach, heal, cast our evil spirits, and make disciples.
Pentecost: The Apostles' and disciples' baptism with the Holy Spirit.	Following Jesus' resurrection, and prior to Pentecost, there is no record of the Apostles engaging in ministry. They tarried in prayer in Jerusalem, waiting like seeds in the soil to be quickened with life. They waited like sails on a ship to be filled with wind.	The Holy Spirit quickened the seed. He filled their sails with wind. The Holy Spirit empowered them to dynamically advance the gospel. The Holy Spirit enabled them to speak powerful words and to perform mighty works (signs and wonders) that verified that their message was true.
Our baptism with the Holy Spirit.	Functional gifts of the Spirit evident (Romans 12:3-8)	Manifestational gifts of the Spirit released (1 Cor. 12:7ff.)

Terminology

When referring to the Holy Spirit's <u>initial</u> work of empowerment in our lives, it is probably wisest to use the phrase *baptized with the Holy Spirit* (Mark 1:7-8; Luke 3:16; John 1:32-33; Acts 1:4-5; Acts 11:15-16). We are initiated into the power dimension of ministry when we are baptized with the Holy Spirit.

Based on the examples that follow, it is appropriate to use a variety of other words and phrases to describe <u>subsequent experiences</u> of empowerment. Examples:

- She/he was <u>filled with</u> the Holy Spirit (Luke 1:41-42; 1:67-68; Acts 2:4; 4:7-8; 4:31; 9:17; 13:8-9).
- The Holy Spirit <u>came on or upon</u> him/her/me (Luke 2:25; 4:18; Acts 1:8; 19:5-6).
- Jesus <u>poured out</u> the Holy Spirit upon him/her/us (Acts 2:33).
- The Holy Spirit <u>fell on</u> him/her/them (Acts 8:16; 10:44).
- He/she/we received a <u>fresh infilling</u> with the Holy Spirit (Acts 8:17).
- He/she/we received a <u>fresh anointing</u> (Acts 10:38).
- He/she/we <u>received the Holy Spirit</u> (Acts 10:47).

R.A. Torrey elaborated by saying:

> The baptism with the Holy Spirit is a definite experience of which one may and ought to know whether he has received it or not. ... A man may be regenerated by the Holy Spirit and still not be baptized with the Holy Spirit. ... The baptism with the Holy Spirit is an operation of the Holy Spirit distinct from

and subsequent and additional to His regenerating work. In regeneration there is an impartation of life, and the one who receives it is saved; in the baptism with the Holy Spirit there is an impartation of power and the one who receives it is fitted for service. ...

"Baptized with the Holy Spirit," "Filled with the Holy Spirit," "The Holy Ghost fell on them," "The gift of the Holy Ghost was poured out," "Received the Holy Ghost," "I send the promise of my Father upon you," "Endued with power from on high," are used in the New Testament to describe one and the same experience.[43]

---

[43] Zeb Bradford Long and Douglas McMurry, *Gateways to Empowered Ministry* (The Dunamis Project, PRMI.org, Revised 2006), 211. Drawn from R.A. Torrey, *What the Bible Teaches About the Holy Spirit* (NY: Revel, 1898), 271.

Chapter 14: Repeating Pentecost

Each major expansion of the gospel in the Book of Acts included a passing-on of the empowering work of the Holy Spirit to new groups of believers so that they, too, will be equipped to fulfill our Acts 1:8 mandate. Being empowered by the Holy Spirit was (and, is) important to God.

We tend to think, "Hallelujah! They accepted Christ. Let's add a little discipleship and that's all they need." But in Acts, Jesus consistently orchestrated one more step, namely baptism with the Holy Spirit.

1. "Pentecosts" in the New Testament: An Overview

1	Jesus' "Pentecost"	Jordan River	Mt. 3:13-17
2	Apostle's Pentecost	Jerusalem	Acts 2:1-4
3	Samaritan "Pentecost"	Samaria	Acts 8:4-25
4	Saul's "Pentecost"	Damascus	Acts 9:1-19
5	Gentile "Pentecost"	Cornelius in Caesarea	Acts 10:1-48; 11:1-18
6	Ephesian "Pentecost"	Ephesus	Acts 19:1-7
7	Your personal "Pentecost"		

Each experience of empowerment proved to be a "hinge event" in the recipient's life. In some instances, but not all, the Biblical narrative describes how the trajectory of their lives changed following their baptism with the Holy Spirit. Note, for example, that Jesus' public ministry did not begin until after His baptism with the Holy Spirit. Jesus' baptism was a "hinge event" in His life. Before, He did not teach or perform miracles. After, He went forth in the power of the Holy Spirit (Luke 4:14), preaching, teaching, healing, and driving out evil spirits.

Likewise, our baptism with the Holy Spirit will be a hinge event in our lives. Additional "fillings" will follow as needed.

"PENTECOSTS" IN THE NEW TESTAMENT

"Pentecosts" in the New Testament included:

A. An address (a location such as the Jordan River, Jerusalem, Samaria, Damascus, Caesarea, Ephesus); and, in most cases,

B. A spiritual "midwife" or "igniter," or "fire starter" that is, a person or team through whom Jesus poured out the Holy Spirit (Philip, Ananias, Peter, Paul).

Between now and when Jesus returns, many more "pentecosts" – i.e., great awakenings, outpourings of the Holy Spirit – will occur. Each will have an address and an igniter (an individual or team).

I wonder who God is raising up in our day for this purpose. I wonder where He will work next …

1. Jesus' "Pentecost" at the Jordan River, Matthew 3:13-17

> *Then Jesus came from Galilee to the Jordan to John, to be baptized by him. 14 John would have prevented him, saying, "I need to be baptized by you, and do you come to me?" 15 But Jesus answered him, "Let it be so now, for thus it is fitting for us to fulfill all righteousness." Then he consented. 16 And when Jesus was baptized, immediately he went up from the water, and behold, the heavens were opened to him, and he saw the Spirit of God descending like a dove and coming to rest on him; 17 and behold, a voice from heaven said, "This is my beloved Son, with whom I am well pleased."* Matthew 3:13-17, ESV

As we noted above, Jesus' public ministry did not begin until after His baptism with the Holy Spirit. Before it He did not teach or perform miracles. After He went forth in the power of the Holy Spirit (Luke 4:14), preaching, teaching, healing, and driving out demons.

2. The Apostle's Pentecost in Jerusalem, Acts 2:1-4

> *When the day of "Pentecost" arrived, they were all together in one place. 2 And suddenly there came from heaven a sound like a mighty rushing wind, and it filled the entire house where they were sitting. 3 And divided tongues as of fire appeared to them and rested on each one of them. 4 And they were all filled with the Holy Spirit and began to speak in other tongues as the Spirit gave them utterance.* Acts 2:1-4, ESV

Following Jesus' resurrection, the disciples' public ministry did not begin until after they were baptized with the Holy Spirit. Their baptism with the Holy Spirit was a "hinge event," that is, a turning point, in their lives. What happened next?

- Anointed words   Acts 2:14-36
- Mighty works   Acts 3:1-10

3. The Samaritan's "Pentecost," Acts 8:4-25

> *Now those who were scattered went about preaching the word. 5 Philip went down to the city of Samaria and proclaimed to them the Christ. 6 And the crowds with one accord paid attention to what was being said by Philip when they heard him and saw the signs that he did. 7 For unclean spirits, crying out with a loud voice, came out of many who had them, and many who were paralyzed or lame were healed. 8 So there was much joy in that city. Acts 8:4-8, ESV*

Q: Why did the crowd pay attention to Philip?
A: Because they heard him preach and saw the signs that he did.

Response: Simon the Magician and others became believers.

> *There was a man named Simon, who had previously practiced magic in the city and amazed the people of Samaria, saying that he himself was somebody great. 10 They all paid attention to him, from the least to the greatest, saying, "This man is the power of God that is called Great." 11 And they paid attention to him because for a long time he had amazed them with his magic.*

*But when they <u>believed</u> Philip as he preached good
news about the kingdom of God and the name of Jesus
Christ, <u>they were baptized</u>, both men and
women. 13 Even Simon himself <u>believed</u>, and after
being baptized he continued with Philip. And seeing
signs and great miracles performed, he was amazed.
Acts 8:9-13, ESV*

Q: What type of baptism occurred in Acts 8:12?
A: Believers' baptism in water. Faith and water baptism went
hand-in-hand.

*Now when the apostles at Jerusalem heard
that Samaria had <u>received the word</u> of God, they sent to
them Peter and John ... Acts 8:14, ESV*

Q: What is the meaning of "received" (*dexaomai*) in 8:14?
A: "Received the word" in this context means that the
Samaritans heard the good news (Acts 8:12), believed it (Acts
8:12), and were baptized (Acts 8:12). Acts 8:12 references the
Samaritan's conversion. cf. John 1:12.

Note carefully what happened next.

*Now when the apostles at Jerusalem heard
that Samaria had <u>received the word</u> of God, they sent to
them Peter and John who came down* [i.e., Peter and
John traveled from Jerusalem to Samaria] *and prayed
for them that they might <u>receive</u> the Holy
Spirit, 16 for he <u>had not yet fallen on</u> any of them,
but they had only been baptized in the name of the Lord
Jesus. 17 Then they laid their hands on them and they
<u>received</u> the Holy Spirit. Acts 8:15-17, ESV*

Q: What is the meaning of "received" (*lambanw*) in Acts 8:15, 17, 19?

A: In these verses "received" is a reference to the Holy Spirit falling *on* them (Acts 8:16), i.e., to baptism with the Holy Spirit. In Acts 8:15, 17, 19, "received" links to the empowering dimension of the Holy Spirit's work.

Point and Implications

Receiving the Holy Spirit for salvation was good but not good enough. The Apostles insisted on facilitating one more important spiritual transaction, not to secure the Samaritan's salvation but to equip them to witness and serve with greater effectiveness (Acts 1:8). They sent Peter and John to pray for the new converts to receive the Holy Spirit's empowerment.

For Reflection:

How often do we determine that conversion is sufficient? How often do we take the next step and pray for empowerment for the new converts?

4. Saul's "Pentecost," Acts 9:17-19

> *So Ananias departed and entered the house. And laying his hands on him he said, "Brother Saul, the Lord Jesus who appeared to you on the road by which you came has sent me so that you may regain your sight and be <u>filled</u> [pim-play-me] with the Holy Spirit." 18 And immediately something like scales fell from his eyes, and he regained his sight. Then he rose and was baptized; 19 and taking food, he was strengthened.*
> Acts 9:17-19, ESV

Ananias did not pray for Saul's salvation because Saul had already been converted on the road to Damascus. Rather, Ananias prayed for Saul to regain his sight and be "filled" (*pim-play-me*) with the Holy Spirit.

"*Pim-play-me*" in Luke and Acts refers consistently to a short-term filling with the Holy Spirit leading to dramatic action. It is another way of pointing to the empowering dimension of the Holy Spirit's work. See Luke 1:41-42, Luke 1:67, Acts 2:4, Acts 4:8, Acts 4:31, Acts 9:17-18, and Acts 13:9-10. Hence, Ananias prayed for the Holy Spirit to fall upon Saul and empower him for witness and service.

This encounter proved to be a "hinge event" in Saul's life. Following this, Saul/Paul became a key leader in the early church, writing thirteen letters which continue to shape our lives today.

5. Gentile's "Pentecost," Acts 10:44-48. Cornelius in Caesarea

Cornelius was a Roman centurion, a commander of 100 soldiers in the Italian Regiment of the Roman military. He lived in Caesarea. Cornelius was a generous gentile who feared God (Acts 10:1-2) but did not have a personal relationship with God. He invited Peter to travel from Joppa to Caesarea and speak to his household.

> *While Peter was still saying these things, the Holy Spirit fell on all who heard the word. Acts 10:44, ESV*

fell on is the language of empowerment. That this is Peter's meaning is made clear in the next two verses (Acts 10:45-46).

> *45 And the believers from among the circumcised who had come with Peter were amazed, because the <u>gift of the Holy Spirit was poured out</u> even on the Gentiles. [44] 46 For they were hearing them <u>speaking in tongues and extolling God.</u>* Acts 10:45-46, ESV

On the Day of Pentecost, the same pattern occurred in Acts 2:4. This is clearly evidence of the Holy Spirit's empowering work on the Gentiles.

> *Then Peter declared, 47 "Can anyone withhold water for baptizing these people, who have <u>received[45] the Holy Spirit just as we have?"</u> 48 And he commanded them to be baptized in the name of Jesus Christ. Then they asked him to remain for some days.*
> Acts 10:46-48, ESV

The Gentiles received the Holy Spirit for salvation and for empowerment on the same occasion. For some of us likewise, salvation and empowerment occur on the same occasion.

Please notice: God could have been satisfied with a dramatic conversion experience for the Gentiles, but He arranged for more: He also sent the Holy Spirit to empower the Gentiles for effective witness and service.

---

[44] Cf. Peter's report to the believers in Jerusalem in Acts 11:1-18. *As I began to speak, <u>the Holy Spirit fell on them just as on us</u> at the beginning. 16 And I remembered the word of the Lord, how he said, 'John baptized with water, but you will be <u>baptized with the Holy Spirit.</u>' 17 If then God gave the same gift to them as he gave to us when we believed in the Lord Jesus Christ, who was I that I could stand in God's way?"* Acts 11:15-17, ESV

[45] The meaning of "receive" here parallels the meaning of "receive" in Acts 8:17 and 19:2.

6. The Ephesians' "Pentecost," Acts 19:1-7

> *It happened that while Apollos was at Corinth, Paul*
> *passed through the inland country and came to*
> *Ephesus. There he found some <u>disciples</u>. 2 And he said*
> *to them, "Did you <u>receive</u> the Holy Spirit when you*
> *believed?"*
> *And they said, "No, we have not even heard that there*
> *is a Holy Spirit."*
> *3 And he said, "Into what then were you baptized?"*
> *They said, "Into John's baptism."*
> *4 And Paul said, "John baptized with the baptism of*
> *repentance, telling the people to believe in the one who*
> *was to come after him, that is, Jesus."*
> *5 On hearing this, they were <u>baptized in the name of the</u>*
> *<u>Lord Jesus</u>.* Acts 19:1-5, ESV

Paul used the word "disciples" to describe the people he met in
Ephesus (19:1). Who were these disciples following? John the
Baptist (19:3-4). After Paul told them about Jesus, they were
baptized in the name of the Lord Jesus (19:5): they became
Christians. Their baptism in water marked their conversion /
salvation / regeneration.

Paul asked the disciples in 19:2 *"Did you <u>receive</u> the Holy*
Spirit when you believed?"? As noted above in the discussion
regarding the Samaritans' "Pentecost" (Acts 8:4-25),
sometimes the word "receive" refers to salvation, and other
times, to empowerment. It has a dual meaning. In Acts 19:1-7,
Paul has in mind receiving the Holy Spirit for empowerment.

Please note again: Paul was not content to say, "You have been
baptized in the Name of Jesus, and now you are now
Christians. Great! I will report this good news to the Apostles
in Jerusalem." Rather Paul proceeded intentionally to invite the
Holy Spirit to empower them to be Christ's witnesses. Paul laid

hands on them and the Holy Spirit came upon them in power. Evidence: They began speaking in tongues and prophesying.

> *When Paul had laid his hands on them, the Holy Spirit came <u>on</u> them, and <u>they began speaking in tongues and prophesying.</u>* Acts 19:6, ESV

While serving at the Chinese Community Church in San Diego, we followed a similar pattern. Whenever we baptized a person, while they stood soak-and-wet in the baptismal, one or two of the ministry leaders joined with me in laying hands on them and calling on the Holy Spirit to come upon them, awaken their spiritual gifts, and empower them for effective witness and service.

Paul's question to the Ephesians is a fitting question for each of us.

> *"Did you receive the Holy Spirit when you believed?"* Acts 19:2, ESV.

George O. Wood underscored the purpose of empowerment when he wrote:

> Spirit baptism is an initial event meant to propel us into empowerment to bear witness. There must not only be initial evidence of being baptized in the Spirit; there must be continuing evidence of a Spirit-empowered life. A Pentecostal church that is not reaching people for Jesus is a contradiction in terms. We were never formed to be a small group that gathers and says, "Here we are, Lord – bless us." No! Like Abraham, we are called to bless the world. There is a great, unfinished Commission to take the gospel to all the unreached peoples of the earth."[46]

Summation

1. Each major expansion of the gospel included a passing-on of the empowering work of the Holy Spirit to the new group of believers so that each would be equipped to fulfill our Acts 1:8 mandate.

2. Being empowered by the Holy Spirit was (and, is) important to God.

Standing on the Shoulders of Spiritual Giants

In presenting this perspective I stand on the shoulders of spiritual giants such as R.A. Torrey, D.L. Moody, and Brad Long. Our view is that baptism with the Holy Spirit ...

*   Is an operation of the Holy Spirit that is distinct from, and in addition to, His works of regeneration and sanctification.

*   May or may not be accompanied by speaking in tongues.

*   Equips and releases believers to witness and serve with greater effectiveness.

*   Is available to all believers.

---

[46] George O. Wood, "Marks of the Assemblies," (Charisma Magazine, 2014), 34. See also R.A. Torrey, *The Holy Spirit: Who He Is and What He Does* (Classic Books for Today, NO. 152, 2000), 39.

In a real sense, baptism with the Holy Spirit *is* a second blessing but its purpose is not to impart holiness; rather, to equip with power to witness and serve (Acts 1:8). Further, it is, as Torrey wrote, a "definite experience of which one may and ought to know whether he has received it or not."[47] Those who have been baptized with the Holy Spirit experience Him in greater fullness. They often receive a heightened awareness of Jesus' presence in their lives, as well as an anointing for a special work. Baptism with the Holy Spirit is a gateway not to holiness but to empowerment.

R.A. Torrey made a distinction between his teaching and themes in the Holiness and Pentecostal Movements when he wrote:

> The purpose of the baptism with the Holy Spirit is not primarily to make believers individually holy. I do not say that it is not the work of the Holy Spirit to make believers holy, for as we have already seen, He is "the Spirit of holiness," and the only way we shall ever attain to holiness is by His power. I do not even say that the baptism with the Holy Spirit will not result in a great spiritual transformation and uplift and cleansing … but the primary purpose of the baptism with the Holy Spirit is efficiency in testimony and service.[48]

D.L. Moody observed that,

> In some sense, and to some extent, the Holy Spirit dwells in every believer, but there is another gift which may be called the gift of the Holy Spirit for service.

[47] R.A. Torrey, *The Person and Work of the Holy Spirit* (Grand Rapids, MI: Zondervan, 1910, 1974).

[48] R.A. Torrey, *The Person and Work of the Holy Spirit* (Grand Rapids, MI: Zondervan, 1910, 1974), 155-156.

This gift, it strikes me, is entirely distinct and separate from conversion and assurance. God has a great many children who have no power, and the reason is, they have not the gift of the Holy Ghost for service. … They have not sought this gift."[49]

John Piper stated succinctly,

I think the essence of being baptized with the Holy Spirit is when a person, who is already a believer, receives extraordinary spiritual power for Christ-exalting ministry.[50]

A.W. Tozer wrote,

I want here boldly to assert that it is my happy belief that every Christian can have a copious [bountiful] outpouring of the Holy Spirit in a measure far beyond that received at conversion.[51]

Baptism with the Holy Spirit as a sovereign work of the Holy Spirit that equips and empowers individuals to carry out their God-given assignments, the first and foremost of which is pointing people to Jesus.

In my opinion, some people have been baptized with the Holy Spirit and do not know it. Their theological framework prevents them from using that phrase to describe their personal and powerful encounter with Jesus Christ, through the Holy Spirit, that changed the trajectory of their lives.

---

[49] Catherine Marshall, *The Helper* (Avon Books, 1978), 60.

[50] http://www.desiringgod.org/library/sermons/90/092390.html

[51] *A.W. Tozer, Tozer on the Holy Spirit: A 366-Day Devotional Compiled by Marilynne E. Foster, 2007)*, entry for November 24.

All God's blessings are good! Let's open our lives to Jesus to be blessed by Him, through the Holy Spirit, not just once or twice, but again … and again … and again.

Chapter 15: Baptism with the Holy Spirit: Real People, Real Stories

In many Christian circles, leaders are very reluctant to include teaching regarding the "baptism with the Holy Spirit" because they view it as divisive. Several years ago, I was invited to participate in a group that was planning a mission convention. As I listened to their plans, I thought to myself,

> Many of the young men and women who will be attending this convention will be seriously considering involvement in missions. Whether they go into missions or not, they need to be baptized with the Holy Spirit so that they will be equipped and empowered to serve Jesus with even greater effectiveness wherever He sends them.

Eventually I suggested to one of the convention's leaders that we should include a workshop on the baptism with the Holy Spirit. His firm response: "At our conventions we do not permit presenters to teach on that topic. It is too divisive."

Unfortunately, all too often he is correct: teaching on the baptism with the Holy Spirit results in division. But that's not the way it needs to be! A balanced, Biblical understanding of

Spirit-baptism, that is rooted in the Old Testament and flows logically into the New Testament, yields great unity, freedom, and power.

The first time I heard a series of Biblically-balanced teaching on the baptism with the Holy Spirit, I felt angry. "Why," I asked, "didn't someone tell me about this before?!?"

John the Baptist declared, *He [Jesus] will baptize you with the Holy Spirit and fire,* Luke 3:16, ESV. (Parallel: Mark 1:8; Luke 3:16; John 1:32-33). Following His ascension, Jesus Himself used a similar phrase when He commanded His disciples

> *not to depart from Jerusalem, but to wait for the promise of the Father, which, he said, "you heard from me; for John baptized with water, but you will be baptized with the Holy Spirit not many days from now."* Acts 1:4-5, ESV

Individual Christians who are "baptized with the Holy Spirit" are empowered by the Spirit for more effective witness and service. Remember the Old Testament pattern? The Spirit came "upon" or "clothed" individuals and they were enabled to perform mighty works and/or speak powerful words. Similar results occur in our day.

Many years ago, A.W. Tozer observed, "The Spirit-filled life is not a special, deluxe edition of Christianity. It is part and parcel of the total plan of God for His people."[52] To his words I add a hearty "Amen!"

---

[52] A.W. Tozer, *How to be Filled with the Holy Spirit* (Harrisburg, PA: Christian Publications, n.d.).

Phil's Story

During the opening days of a PRMI Dunamis Conference in Muskegon, Michigan, in the year 2000, I listened with a guarded heart to various teachings about the Person and work of the Holy Spirit. Since I considered myself to be a good student of Scripture, I wanted to be certain that what I heard was both grounded in the Word and balanced. It was. I also enjoyed meeting the people who were serving on the leadership team. They were warm, bright, loving, patient with my questions, and full of life. My heart began to hunger for a deeper relationship with the Father, Son, and Holy Spirit.

In September, 2001, I attended another Dunamis Conference. On the final evening, after prayer teams fanned out around the perimeter of the room, we were encouraged to approach one or more of the teams and to receive prayer. Initially, I approached a team that included Brad. In the midst of this time of prayer, Brad paused and spoke prophetically over me, saying, "I see the Lord giving you discernment into what is happening in churches and communities." A moment later, he said, "I see you fighting your way through the underbrush and up a mountain. You reach a clearing and look back, and many people are following you."

That was a new experience! However, even though it seemed right and fitting, that was not my baptism with the Holy Spirit.

A little later that evening, I approached another team that included Victor Matthews and Jon DeBruyn. Victor prayed that if I did not yet have the gift of tongues, I would receive it. [I didn't … at least not exactly. More on that later.] Victor and Jon prayed for the Holy Spirit to come "upon" me and anoint me with power. In faith, I believed and received the baptism with the Holy Spirit. The only indication that the Holy Spirit might be at work in my life came the next morning during an exalted time of worship. As we worshipped, I felt a subtle "pressure" or "wind" on my back, and a gentle, joyous, short-lived bubbling-up in my stomach. (No, it was not indigestion.)

Since I did not experience any obvious, objective, or lasting manifestations of the Spirit, I left the Conference wondering if the Spirit-baptism, of which Scripture speaks and for which I hungered, had really occurred in my life.

When I returned to Traverse City, Michigan, I felt compelled to take long walks in the woods behind our home – specifically, on the trails surrounding the Mt. Holiday Snow Ski Resort, as well as on the shores of East Bay – in order to be alone in God's presence. In a manner that had not occurred in my life prior to that point, praise and worship flowed freely – sometimes gushing forth powerfully – from my inner man. As I walked, I cried out over and over again, "Jesus, baptize me with the Holy Spirit!" After approximately ten days of praising Jesus and crying out to Him to "baptize me with the Holy Spirit," I heard Him quietly whisper deep within, "I already have."

Since that day, one of my repeated prayers for myself has been this:

> Lord Jesus Christ, fill me afresh and anew with the Holy Spirit empowering me for ministry in general and for every specific ministry to which you are calling me today.

I am learning by trial and error to stay in step with the Spirit – to join the "dance of cooperation" with the Father, Son, and Holy Spirit, and I am deeply grateful to God for His patient and continuing work in me and through me.

Baptism with the Holy Spirit: More Stories ...

Jesus told stories to instruct and inspire, and they have the same impact on us today. Each story that follows chronicles the Holy Spirit's beautiful, dynamic, and variegated work in the lives of His children.

Joanne's Story[53]

Joanne lives in Edmonton, Alberta, Canada. She participates on the prayer ministry team in her church and serves on the leadership team for Dunamis, Canada. She and her husband, Curt, love to cycle. Here is her story.

I [Joanne] grew up in a home where we were always going to church. Eventually, as an adult in my 30's, something began to stir in me and I thought, "There must be more to the Christian life than I am experiencing." Reading the Book of Acts only intensified my thirst and frustration because I did not see any action like that in my life or circle of friends.

One Sunday I read an announcement in our bulletin that Brad Long would be teaching at a nearby church on the Holy Spirit. Immediately I wanted to attend because I was seeking greater understanding about the role of the Holy Spirit in our lives today. I went excited and fearful, and my husband, Curt, went with me. Before the evening was over, Curt had a vision, which was a really new experience for him! Even though nothing at all happened in my life, I continued to have an inner drive to learn more. We became a conference junkies and went to every group I could find that talked about the Holy Spirit. In time my daughter-in-law invited me to attend a Woman's Aglow

---

[53] Joanne's story is also included in my book, *A Primer on the Empowering Work of the Holy Spirit.*.

conference near my home in Edmonton, Alberta, Canada. A compelling speaker shared a dream she had about a big library. In the dream God put His finger on one line in one book and said, "This is all you know about Me." "You're right!" I said to myself. "God is so big! and I know so little about Him."

In my church, prayer was not evident other than during the service, but at this Woman's Aglow meeting, everyone around me respond to the invitation for prayer. So I got in line. As my line inched forward I thought to myself, "What will I ask for? I'm not even sure why I'm in line." When I stood before the prayer ministry team, they asked how they could pray for me. To my surprise I heard myself say, "Surrender." As soon as they began to pray for me, something shifted deep within me and I received the gift of tongues. I certainly was not seeking that gift, and since I was from a Christian Reformed Church background, this was a shock! They continued to pray for me and next thing I knew I was resting in the Spirit on the floor. Unbelievable! The ladies wisely counseled me to just rest for a little while longer and let the Holy Spirit work in me. They hovered near and kept praying, and I really appreciated that.

Before I drove home that evening I called Curt and told him, "You'll never believe what happened to me! They prayed for me and I received the gift of tongues!" His response really surprised me and warmed my heart. "I've been praying for you all day that you would."

Providentially, the ladies who prayed for me had warned me that the enemy would mess with my mind. Sure enough, he did. As I drove home questions came such as, "Did I just make that up? Did that really happen?" Within moments the Holy Spirit assured me, "No that was really real."

The next morning we went to our home church and my heart experienced times of refreshing. Tears filled my eyes as we

sang the same old hymns that I had sung for years. To my
surprise I heard myself singing in tongues! Curt heard me too
and smiled knowingly. At the end of the service I told a trusted
wise man in our congregation who was Spirit filled, what was
happening. He was overjoyed. However, I did not say much of
anything to anyone else for about three years. I wanted to learn
more before making my new-found relationship with the Holy
Spirit public.

Eventually the Lord led me to attend a series of Dunamis
Conferences sponsored by Presbyterian Reformed Ministries
International, the organization where Brad Long was the
Executive Director. Very helpful! In time I invited others from
our church who I sensed were thirsting for more of Jesus to
join me. One lady resisted somewhat saying, "I will come with
you as long as there's no fu-fu." Although I was not sure what
she meant by "fu-fu," I responded, "Just come." She did, and
so did 8-10 others. My friend is now a Spirit-filled point person
for the prayer ministry in our church. Today the prayer culture
of our church is changing for good, praise God!

Dr. Reuben Archer Torrey's Story[54]

R.A. Torrey's (1856-1928) credentials are remarkable. He was
a rich man's son, a college graduate, and an intellectual who,
after studying theology at Yale, Leipzig and Erlangen, read the
New Testament in Greek each day and the Old Testament in
Hebrew. D. L. Moody chose Torrey to serve as the
superintendent of the Bible Institute in Chicago, known today
as Moody Bible Institute. If this scholar and educator needed to
be baptized with the Holy Spirit, how much more do we!

---

[54] Torrey's story is also included in my book, *A Primer on the Empowering
Work of the Holy Spirit*.

I (Dr. Torrey) had been a minister for some years before I came
to the place where I saw that I had no right to preach until I
was definitely baptized with the Holy Ghost. I went to a
business friend of mine and said to him in private, "I am never
going to enter my pulpit again until I have been baptized with
the Holy Spirit and know it, or until God in some way tells me
to go." Then, just as far as I could, I shut myself up alone in my
study and spent the time continually on my knees asking God
to baptize me with the Holy Spirit. As the days passed, the
devil tried to tempt me by saying, "Suppose Sunday comes and
you are not baptized with the Holy Spirit, what then?" I replied,
"Whatever comes, I will not go into my pulpit and preach again
until I have been baptized with the Holy Spirit and know it, or
God in some way tells me to go; even though I have to tell my
people that I have never been fit to preach." But Sunday did not
come before the blessing came. I had it more or less definitely
mapped out in my mind what would happen; but what I had
mapped out in my mind did not happen. I recall the exact spot
where I was kneeling in prayer in my study. I could go to the
very spot in that house at 1348 N. Adams Street in
Minneapolis. It was a very quiet moment, one of the most quiet
moments I ever knew; indeed, I think one reason I had to wait
so long was because it took that long before my soul could get
quiet before God. Then God simply said to me, not in any
audible voice, but in my heart, "It's yours. Now go and
preach."[55]

Sometime after this experience (I do not recall just how long
after), while sitting in my room one day, that very same room, I
recall just where I was sitting, before my revolving bookcase, I
do not know whether I was thinking about this subject at all, I
do not remember, but suddenly as near as I can describe it,
though it does not exactly describe it, I was struck from my

---

[55] Reuben Archer Torrey, *The Holy Spirit: Who He Is and What He Does*
(Classic Books for Today, NO. 152, 2000), 54-55.

chair on to the floor and I found myself shouting (I was not brought up to shout and I am not of a shouting temperament, but I shouted like the loudest shouting Methodist) "glory to God, glory to God, glory to God," and I could not stop. I tried to stop, but it was just as if some other power than my own was moving my jaws. At last, when I had succeeded in pulling myself together, I went downstairs and told my wife what had happened.

But that was not when I was baptized with the Holy Spirit. I was baptized with the Holy Spirit when I took Him by simple faith in the naked Word of God, and anyone of you can be thus baptized today, yes, you can be thus baptized before you leave this building this afternoon.[56]

Dwight L. Moody's Story

D. L. Moody (1837-1899) served as one of America's greatest evangelists as well as the founder of Moody Bible Institute in Chicago. Moody and Dr. R.A. Torrey were close friends and coworkers. In his small book, *Why God Used D.L. Moody,* Torrey wrote about "the definite enduement from on high" that empowered Moody's preaching.[57]

In his early days, Moody, by his own admission was a hustler who worked largely in the energy of his flesh. Two humble, Free Methodist women frequently attended his meetings, sat in the front row, and prayed for him. That nettled Moody; he thought that they should be praying for the lost, not for him. They told him that they were praying for the Holy Spirit's power for him. Eventually Moody asked them to tell him what

---

[56] Ibid., 55.
[57] See http://www.internetmonk.com/archive/d-l-moody-and-the-holy-spirit

they meant, and they told him about the baptism with the Holy Ghost. They prayed together and parted ways.

Not long after, Moody was walking up Wall Street in New York, and the power of God fell upon him. He hurried off to the house of a friend and asked for a room by himself. In that room he stayed alone for hours.

> The Holy Ghost came upon him filling his soul with such joy that at last he had to ask God to withhold His hand lest he die on the spot from very joy. Following his baptism with the Holy Spirit in New York, Moody went on to England for what was to be the first of many evangelistic campaigns there. People thronged to North London to hear him. "The sermons were not different," Moody summarized. "I did not present any new truths, and yet hundreds were converted." The evangelist went on to live another 28 years, and "to reduce the population of hell by a million souls."[58]

Torrey told a story about a meeting that he and Moody had with some fine teachers from Northfield, who believed that every child of God was already baptized with the Holy Ghost at the time of their salvation.

> Mr. Moody came to me and said: "Torrey, will you come up to my house after the meeting tonight and I will get those men to come, and I want you to talk this thing out with them." Of course, I very readily consented, and Mr. Moody and I talked for a long time, but they did not altogether see eye to eye with us. And when they went, Mr. Moody signaled me to remain for a few moments. Mr. Moody sat there with his chin on

---

[58] See http://www.internetmonk.com/archive/d-l-moody-and-the-holy-spirit; and Catherine Marshall, *The Helper* (Avon Books, 1978), 25-26.

his breast, as he so often sat when he was in deep thought; then he looked up and said: "Oh, why will they split hairs? Why don't they see that this is just the one thing that they themselves need?"[59]

Blaise Pascal
November 23, 1654

From about half-past ten in the evening till about half-past twelve – *FIRE!*[60]

Charles Finney's Story

Charles Finney (1792-1875) was an American Presbyterian minister and a leader in the Second Great Awakening in the United States. Regarding his baptism with the Holy Spirit, Finney wrote:

As I turned and was about to take a seat by the fire, I received a mighty baptism of the Holy Ghost. Without any expectation of it, without ever having the thought in my mind that there was any such thing for me, without any recollection that I had ever heard the thing mentioned by any person in the world, the Holy Spirit descended upon me in a manner that seemed to go through me, body and soul. I could feel the impression, like a wave of electricity, going through and through me. Indeed, it seemed to come in waves and waves of liquid love for I could not express it in any other way. It seemed like the very breath of God. I can

---

[59] See http://www.internetmonk.com/archive/d-l-moody-and-the-holy-spirit
[60] J.I. Packer, *Keep In Step With the Spirit* (Baker Books, 2005), 78.

recollect distinctly that it seemed to fan me,
like immense wings.

No words can express the wonderful love that was shed
abroad in my heart. I wept aloud with joy and love; and
I do not know but I should say, I literally bellowed out
the unutterable gushings of my heart. These waves
came over me, and over me, and over me, one after the
other, until I recollect I cried out, "I shall die if these
waves continue to pass over me. I said, "Lord, I cannot
bear any more; yet I had no fear of death. [61]

Jay Knoblock's Story

I (Jay) grew up in an ultra-conservative, legalistic Christian
environment. While I tried to be good, I never found Christ and
was turned off by the "religious spirit" I saw and experienced.
Hence, during college I entered into a period of rebellion. After
getting sick of the shallow relationships and the brokenness of
sin in my life and all around me, I surrendered to Jesus Christ
as Lord and Savior in January of 2006, at the age of 21.

My first year in the Christian faith was all about shedding the
incorrect religious mindset I had and growing in understanding
of who God really was. About 13 months into my walk, I was
baptized in water. About 18 months after I was saved, I was in
China on a college study trip. In Beijing, I took a day to visit a
missionary from my hometown and some of her Chinese
Christian friends. I still remember one of the Christian men
saying to me, "Together we conquer the world for Christ."
This put an excitement in me for missions that remains to this
day.

---

[61] See http://www.patheos.com/blogs/adrianwarnock/2005/05/finneys-experience-of-baptism-in-the-holy-spirit/

After returning from my trip, I spent my last year of college looking into ministry options, witnessing to fellow college students, and studying spiritual things. At that time I felt called to do student ministry after college but had a lot of fears and experienced opposition from some close to me as I tried to go forward. A personal mentor of mine invited me to a Dunamis Conference entitled "Spiritual Warfare," led by Presbyterian-Reformed Ministries International. I was hesitant to go because I knew the group was Charismatic and I didn't fully trust that sort of thing. But God gave me a puzzling vision a week before the conference, and I decided to go to see if they would interpret it.

The conference was very perplexing for me. I heard people quietly praying around the room, and they seemed to be making mysterious "clicking" noises. Was this tongues? I wasn't sure. They all seemed so happy and joyful – even at a spiritual warfare conference. It was like they knew God in a way I did not. I was told to go to an extra session called "Gateways Makeup." I didn't go because I was already overwhelmed with the stress of my future and all of this new "weird" stuff. But I did receive prayer ministry regarding my vision. That prayer time turned into a whole lot more than I ever dreamed it would and was very emotional for me. I had a vision of Jesus bringing healing to things from my past. Again, I was awed by how these people "knew" to ask the questions that they did. It was like God was guiding them or something.

The final night of the event, I went forward for prayer. They asked if I had ever been "baptized with the Holy Spirit." I shared that I had been baptized in water in the name of the Father, Son, and Holy Spirit. They explained that this was something a bit different and that it would prepare me for the ministry God was calling me to. I agreed, but was fearful that I might speak in tongues or get into demonic things. After they prayed, I felt very heavy and began to stagger. Eventually, they told me to "Let it go" and I rested in the Spirit on the floor. I wasn't sure about all of this, but I couldn't deny something had happened.

Before I left, I was given a book called *Receiving the Power*. To be nice I took it but wasn't really interested in reading it, so it was shelved and I forgot all about it. I went through a very hard time after that and experienced a lot of spiritual warfare. I got confused and was very depressed. The mission training I received did not stop the pain, and I ended up deciding I could not do ministry at that time. It was a terrible time in my life and I don't know how I survived that summer.

The next fall, the depression lifted and I began to walk forward with the Lord. I remember doing more witnessing and it was somehow different than before. I had such love for the people I talked to and I didn't seem to care so much about having a perfect format before I went out. God just gave me the words. It was weird.

The following spring I ended up going to South Korea to teach English for a year. For some reason, I brought along the book *Receiving the Power*. During the summer of 2009, I read the book and began to understand what had happened to me. his time, I fully embraced and received the baptism of the Holy Spirit, and also received the gift of tongues … but I doubted it was really real. I began to have more divine appointments after that as well.

I was still battling a spirit of legalistic religion from my formative years pretty strongly during that time. Gradually I was learning to discern God's voice. I received some powerful prayer at an anointed worship service in Seoul in the spring of 2010. Shortly after that, I forgave those who had hurt me and began to open my heart up more to Jesus. Tongues came through more fully, and my love for people grew significantly. I also began to really enjoy freedom in worship and was able to more clearly discern the voice of the Spirit.

The journey has continued, and today I am privileged to teach many about the baptism of the Holy Spirit. I have been blessed to witness thousands of God-orchestrated events and encounters, salvations, deliverances, and healings, and hundreds and hundreds of prophetic words. Praise God for His patience and grace!

I believe things could have been easier had I attended the Gateways makeup session at the Dunamis Conference I attended or read the book they gave me earlier. I was so confused and either of these would have answered my questions. Still, God worked through it all and my life has been forever changed for the better. To God be the glory!

Michael Cassidy's Story
Cambridge University

[Late one night] sleep would not come to me. Instead, quite out of the blue, the Spirit of praise came upon my soul. All seemed to be release. All seemed to be freedom. Hour after hour I praised my God in unrestrained and unrestrainable doxology and song. In words of men and angels I rejoiced. No fatigue visited me that night. All my senses were vibrantly alive to God. The Holy Spirit was blessing me. Wave upon wave, it seemed. Flow upon flow. He seemed to be bubbling up within, surrounding from without, ascending from below and descending from above. ... Somewhere in the early hours of the morning I said to myself, "I don't know the correct biblical name for this, but this is the experience I've heard others talk of."[62]

128

Francis MacNutt's Story

Francis MacNutt (born 1925) served for a number of years as an American Roman Catholic priest. He wrote:

> In August, 1967, during a conference at Maryville College in Tennessee, my life changed radically when I asked for prayer to receive baptism in the Holy Spirit. When a group prayed for me as if I were to receive the Spirit for the first time, nothing much happened. But the next afternoon, when a few friends prayed for a release in me of the gifts of the Spirit (which I had already received in baptism, confirmation, and ordination), I was overwhelmed with joy, and a wave of laughter swept over me. My life has never been the same.[63]

Baptism with the Holy Spirit: What happens? Power Added

Every person I know who has given serious thought to the Holy Spirit's work of empowerment struggles to put into words the answer to this question: "What happens when we are baptized with the Holy Spirit?" What spiritual transaction occurs when we experience our personal Pentecost? And, what happens spiritually during subsequent experiences of empowerment?

---

[62] David Williams, *Signs, Wonders, and the Kingdom of God* (Vine Books, 1989), 15, quoting Michael Cassidy, "Bursting the Wineskins," 1983, 122.
[63] Francis MacNutt, *Deliverance from Evil Spirits* (Grand Rapids, MI: Chosen Books, 1995), 271.

Honestly, we do not know exactly what happens; there will always be an element of mystery. Nevertheless, I believe that the following statements are a reasonably accurate summary of the spiritual significance of these experiences.

1. Our baptism with the Holy Spirit expands our capacity, giving the Holy Spirit more freedom to work in us and through us. We surrender, and He fills. He surges into us with greater fullness.

Contemplate this parallel: When a person has asthma, he uses an inhaler to create a capacity in his lungs to hold more air. Likewise, when we are baptized with the Holy Spirit, Jesus expands the capacity of our hearts to hold more of the Holy Spirit. However, we do not live in a state of perpetual fullness. As we engage in ministry, the Spirit who fills us flows out from us (see Mark 5:30) to bless, build up, free, heal, and restore others. In our depleted state, we must return to Jesus time and time again for fresh infillings and for fresh anointings with the Holy Spirit.

2. Our baptism with the Holy Spirit equips us to accomplish the work that God the Father desires to do through us. When the Spirit came upon Amasai, he prophesied. When the Spirit came upon Gideon, he rallied the troops and defeated the Midianites. When the Spirit came upon Saul in Acts 9, he received the grace to function as an Apostle to the Gentiles.

When we are baptized with the Holy Spirit, either Jesus activates the gifts He gave us when we initially believed in Him, and/or He downloads (imparts) a fresh set of skills, authority, and power. He equips us to successfully fulfill our God-ordained destiny/calling/mission. Everyone is called to witness. In addition, most people are beckoned to participate in specific short-term or long-term missions:

- Restore marriages
- Shepherd a flock
- Break down strongholds and set captives free
- Lead worship
- Build an orphanage
- Plant a church
- Rescue women
- Intercede for a nation

As a result of the Holy Spirit's anointing, we are better equipped to join the dance of cooperation with the Father, Son, and Holy Spirit, and successfully do what Jesus wants done.

We do not receive our gifts and skills in a fully-developed form. Rather, as time unfolds we must engage with the Holy Trinity to develop the grace we received when we were baptized with the Holy Spirit.

Let's look at baptism with the Holy Spirit from another angle.

When the Holy Spirit comes upon us, are we getting more of the Holy Spirit? Did we have 60% of Him before, and do we get 40% more for the duration of time that He empowers us? Even though Biblical authors do not answer this question, it seems to me that the illustration of a pilot light provides a reasonable explanation. A pilot light is fully a flame but not a full flame. When the thermostat clicks on, more gas is released, resulting in an enlarged flame. It is still a flame, only fuller. Likewise, during moments of empowerment, Jesus turns a valve that enlarges the Spirit's presence in us for the duration of the assignment that He has set before us.

It is not important or necessary for us to understand precisely how the process works. Our role is to surrender to Jesus, allowing Him to transform our candle into a torch.

Chapter 16: Your Personal Pentecost: Preparing for and Receiving Empowerment

Are you ready to embark on a great adventure – an adventure that will thrill your soul … and may cost you more than you ever expected?

The sobering reality of the potential cost associated with the grace of empowerment came home to me in 2001 as I sat quietly on the shore of Lake Michigan and contemplated what I had been learning about the person and work of the Holy Spirit. My heart hungered for more of Jesus and more of His Spirit. In my journal I recorded the following:

> Yesterday, while walking the shores of Lake Michigan following our afternoon session at Dunamis, I asked God to release the manifestational gifts of the Spirit (see 1 Corinthians 12:7-11) to operate in greater measure in me and through me. I sensed in my spirit a deep, clear, and quiet response: "Are you willing to drink the cup which I drink?" I believe that Jesus was saying to me, "Count the cost." I anticipate that spiritual warfare will increase in my life, family, and church. The demands on my schedule will increase. Before I glibly and quickly say "Yes" to Jesus' question, I must count the cost.
>
> Am I willing to "drink the cup"?

"Yes, Lord."

While on the beach, the Lord directed me to ponder this verse:

> The Lord is my strength and my shield; in him
> my heart trusts, and I am helped; my heart
> exults, and with my song I give thanks to him.
> The Lord is the strength of his people; he is the
> saving refuge of his anointed.
> Psalm 28:7-8, ESV

I have come too far to turn back or shift into neutral. "Yes, Lord," I prayed, "Open the floodgates. I ask for a greater release of the manifestational gifts of the Holy Spirit in and through my life in a manner that draws attention to Jesus Christ and exalts Him."

Before the evening meeting started, I called Teri and prayed for protection for her, for us, and for our family.

STEPS TOWARD RECEIVING EMPOWERMENT

Even though there is no set formula or process that we may follow in order to experience the baptism with the Holy Spirit, many people have found guidelines such as the following to be helpful:

1. **Understand that if you are truly a Christian, you already have the Holy Spirit dwelling within you.**

John 14:16; Romans 5:5; 8:9; Galatians 3:2; 4:6; 1
Corinthians 12:13

Here is a helpful distinction:

- The Holy Spirit dwells "within" us to transform us.
- He comes "upon" us to empower and equip us to advance Jesus' agenda.

R.A. Torrey and others (including myself) view empowerment as distinct from regeneration. The purpose of empowerment is not to make us Christians. Nor is it to make us holy or happy. Rather, it is to equip and release us to serve Jesus with greater effectiveness. Torrey wrote:

> In regeneration there is the impartation of life by the Spirit's power, and the one who receives it is saved; in baptism with the Holy Spirit, there is the impartation of power, and the one who receives it is fitted for service.[64]

Jesus Himself did not do any mighty works, such as healing the sick and casting out evil spirits, until after His baptism with the Holy Spirit. In fact, Jesus' ministry of teaching and preaching did not begin until after His water-and-Spirit baptism. Could it be that He was establishing a pattern for us to follow??

2. Understand that you are inadequate.

Randy Clark wrote,

---

[64] Long and McMurry, revised 2006, quoting R.A. Torrey, *The Person and Work of the Holy Spirit*, 1910; 1974, page 211.

I have given much thought to the prerequisite conditions for this spiritual experience of the baptism in the Holy Spirit. ... It seems to me that the first possible condition is to become aware of our personal inadequacy in our Christian life. We must recognize our defeatedness, our indifference, our lack of power, and lack of faith. Second, we must desire for this condition to change. By this I mean we develop a serious desire or hunger to be victorious Christians. Third, we must want our lives to honor God and be used in his service, for his glory. Then, we do not ask for a spiritual high to make us feel good, or for an experience that can boost our ego or spiritual pride. Rather, we are asking for power and gifts to make us commensurate to the task before us of binding the "Strong Man" and plundering his home. ... This empowering enables our faith to express itself in love. [65]

In the late 1800s, D.L. Moody noted:

In some sense, and to some extent, the Holy Spirit dwells in every believer, but there is another gift which may be called the gift of the Holy Spirit for service. This gift, it strikes me, is entirely distinct and separate from conversion and assurance. God has a great many children who have no power, and the reason is, they have not the gift of the Holy Ghost for service. ... They have not sought this gift.[66]

Trying to do the Lord's work in our strength can be exhausting. Jesus declared, *apart from me you can do nothing,* John 15:5, ESV. The prophet Zechariah affirmed, *"Not by might, nor by*

[65] Randy Clark, *Baptism in the Holy Spirit* (Global Awakening, 2011), 29.
[66] Catherine Marshall, *The Helper* (Avon Books, 1978), 60.

power, but by my Spirit," says the Lord of hosts, Zechariah 4:6, ESV.

3. Understand that you are not getting more of the Holy Spirit; rather, you are giving the Holy Spirit more of you.

The more we surrender to Jesus, the more the Holy Spirit fills us and controls us. Dr. R.A. Torrey wisely observed:

> If you think of the Holy Spirit, as so many even among Christian people do today, as a mere influence or power, then your thought will constantly be "How can I get hold of the Holy Spirit and use it?" But if you think of Him in the Biblical way, as a person of divine majesty and glory, your thought will be, "How can the Holy Spirit get hold of me and use me?"[67]

As we noted earlier, Pentecost provides a pattern for empowerment in our day. At *kairos* moments, when our hearts and hands are willing to cooperate with Him, the Holy Spirit, who already lives in us, also, comes upon us. To use an Old Testament analogy, the Holy Spirit clothes Himself with us.[68] As we cooperate with this holy power from on high, God advances His agenda for a particular time and place through us. Once He has accomplished the Father's objective, the Holy Spirit lifts.

Scripture leads us to describe two basic operations of the Holy Spirit:

---

[67] R.A. Torrey, *The Holy Spirit: Who He Is and What He Does* (Classic Books for Today, NO. 152, 2000), 3.
[68] "Clothed" – used of Gideon (Judges 6:34); Amasai (1 Chronicles 12:18); and the disciples (Luke 24:49).

1. The transforming work of the Holy Spirit: Long-term
filling for long-term roles.

The Holy Spirit lives within each and every Christian,
developing Christ-like character qualities - the fruit of the
Spirit. Compelled by Christ's love we do much good and
advance the gospel for the glory of God. This filling includes
the release of the functional gifts of the Spirit recorded in
Romans 12.

2. The empowering work of the Holy Spirit: Short-term filling
for *kairos* moments.

The Holy Spirit rushes upon us. He clothes Himself with us,
thereby equipping us to advance God's agenda for a particular
situation at a particular moment in time. He activates and
releases the spiritual authority, spiritual power, and spiritual
gifts – specifically, one or more of the manifestational gifts of
the Spirit (1 Corinthians 12) – that we need to successfully
fulfill our mission.

In November, 2001, I recorded the following illustration of the
Spirit's empowering work:

> Last night a small group of us gathered in a circle
> around Cindy during a ministry time – at her request –
> to pray for her. I was in a supportive role to Sam, one of
> the Dunamis leaders, who tried several cognitive,
> healing of memories strategies to help Cindy, but
> getting nowhere. As I waited quietly and prayed, the
> Lord put a picture in my mind and nudged me to speak
> it out. "Cindy, walk with Jesus into the garden of your
> life. See him stoop down to pull out the weeds by the
> roots. Now watch as He plants flowers in their place."
> Her excited response: "I can see Him! I can see Him!"

During that moment the Lord appeared to do some significant, deeper healing in her life.

Following our time of prayer, the lady sitting next to me said, "Phil, the Lord's anointing was all over you. If you didn't start to pray, I was going to kick you!" The lady next to her chimed in, "I knew in my spirit that she needed to invite Jesus into the garden with her – and then you began to pray that!"

I am grateful to God for this experience. For months I have taught and believed that there is an inward work of the Spirit for fruit, and an "upon" work – an anointing for ministry where the Holy Spirit comes "upon" a person, ministering powerfully through them – and, when His work is done, He lifts. Last night the Lord allowed me to experience the Spirit "upon" me for ministry.

4. Understand and believe that Jesus' promise of empowerment is for you, too.

The empowering work of the Holy Spirit is for ordinary people like you and me, who are committed to advancing the gospel (Acts 1:8). As we noted before, Peter made this clear when, on the Day of Pentecost, he quoted the Prophet Joel and declared:

> And in the last days it shall be, God declares,
> that I will pour out my Spirit <u>on all</u> flesh,
> and your sons and your daughters shall prophesy,
>   and your young men shall see visions,
>   and your old men shall dream dreams;
> 18 even on my male servants and female servants
>   in those days I will pour out my Spirit, and they shall prophesy. Acts 2:17-18, ESV

The radical implication of Peter's declaration is that empowerment is no longer for a privileged few who are in key leadership roles, as was the case in the Old Testament. Rather, all who hunger may, in faith, receive.

5. Reaffirm your faith in Jesus Christ.

Empowerment is for people who are Christians; i.e., for people who have repented of their sins, placed their faith in Jesus Christ, and are committed to witnessing and serving. When preparing a person to pray to receive the Spirit's baptism, I often suggest – even to people who have been Christians for years – that they once again affirm their faith in Jesus Christ, using words like these:

> Lord Jesus, I believe that You are the Son of God. Thank You for shedding Your blood for the sins of the whole world, and for my sins. I acknowledge that You are my Savior and my Lord.

6. Confess all known sin. Repent.

In contrast to what some people in the Holiness Movement believe, we do not need to be perfect before Jesus will baptize us with the Holy Spirit. Fortunately for us, Jesus is gracious and merciful. However, if we choose to knowingly persist in disobedience in some area(s) of our lives, we cannot expect to receive this grace of empowerment. D. L. Moody reportedly taught that the moment our hearts are emptied of pride, selfish ambition, and everything that is contrary to God's law, the Holy Spirit will fill us full of Himself. However, if we are chock-full of pride, conceit, and worldly ways, there is no room in us for the Spirit of God to work. We must be emptied before we can be filled. The Holy Spirit is Holy, and He functions best in a clean environment.

Ask Jesus to put His finger on areas in your life that are displeasing to Him. When He does, confess them, and turn from (forsake) your sin.

7. Thirst for more of Jesus and more of the Holy Spirit.

On the last day of the feast, the great day, Jesus stood up and cried out, "If anyone thirsts, let him come to me and drink." John 7:37, ESV

- Are you continuing to harbor the illusion that you can fulfill God's calling on your life in your own strength and power?
- Do you hunger for empowerment?
- Do you thirst for the Holy Spirit to come upon you with greater frequency and in greater measure, empowering you for witness and service?
- Is your heart ready to humbly receive?
- Are you eager to "join the dance of cooperation" with the Father, Son, and Holy Spirit?
- Are you thirsting for more love, more power, and more of Jesus in your life?

Realize your utter need for the baptism with the Holy Spirit. Desire it for the glory of God, not your own glory. R.A. Torrey wrote:

> You must desire the baptism with the Holy Spirit in order that you may honor God with more effective service and not merely that you may get a new power or a new influence, or it may [bring] a larger salary.[69]

8. Submit and surrender totally and unconditionally to Jesus Christ.

- Forgive people who have hurt you.
- Renounce Satan's lies.
- Yield control to Jesus.
- Say "No" to pleasurable little sins.
- Let go of your plans for your life.

Again I quote R.A. Torrey:

> This is one of the most fundamental things in receiving the baptism with the Holy Spirit, the unconditional surrender of the will to God. More people miss the baptism with the Holy Spirit at this point, and more people enter experimentally into the baptism with the Holy Spirit at this point than at almost any other.[70]
>
> The power of God is experienced through an act of personal surrender. ... Only by going through a process of dying to self and surrendering one's life to God can we have any hope of experiencing the power of God. ... The power of God is available only to those who surrender their life and will to Him, and allow themselves to go where He leads them and do what He wants them to do.[71]

When we surrender, we say to Jesus, "I am Yours ... totally Yours. I yield my body, mind, will, and emotions to You. Use

---

[69], R.A. Torrey, *The Holy Spirit: Who He Is and What He Does*, 49.
[70] Long and McMurry, *Gateways*, 168.
[71] Ibid, 27.

me as an instrument through whom You play Your music, and as a tool through whom You do Your work in our world."

9. Bind all enemy spirits.

Since religious experiences can come from several sources including the Holy Spirit, evil spirits, other people, and/or ourselves. Hence, it is wise to pray something like this:

> Lord Jesus, on the basis of Your blood shed for our redemption, and Your resurrection power and authority, I ask you to shield me here and now from the adversary and all his associates. I desire to receive and experience only that which You, Jesus, have for me.

10. By faith, ask Jesus to baptize you with the Holy Spirit, and expect to receive.

Be empty. Be open. And ask, definitely ask.

We must appropriate the baptism with the Holy Spirit, and we do so by praying in faith. Dr. Long wrote:

> One receives partly through asking in prayer. The important thing is to ask in prayer. It does not matter what words you use; there are no neat formulas. What matters is the intent of the heart.[72]

Here is Jesus' promise:

> *I tell you, <u>ask, and it will be given to you</u>; seek, and you will find; knock, and it will be opened to you. 10 For <u>everyone who asks receives</u>, and the one who seeks*

---

[72] Long and McMurry, *Gateways*, 288.

finds, and to the one who knocks it will be opened. 11 What father among you, if his son asks for a fish, will instead of a fish give him a serpent; 12 or if he asks for an egg, will give him a scorpion? 13 If you then, who are evil, know how to give good gifts to your children, <u>how much more will the heavenly Father give the Holy Spirit to those who ask him</u>! Luke 11:9-13, ESV

We may be alone in a quiet place when we ask. Or we may be in a crowd. When possible, it is wise to ask a trusted servant of Jesus Christ, who understands the Holy Spirit's work of empowerment and is in a recognized position of spiritual authority, to lay hands on us and pray with us, and for us, to receive. See Acts 9:17; 19:6

Believe that Jesus will answer your prayer.

This is the confidence that we have toward him, that if we ask anything according to his will he hears us. And if we know that he hears us in whatever we ask, we know that we have the requests that we have asked of him. 1 John 5:14-15, ESV

A Prayer for Empowerment

Lord Jesus Christ, I need help. You have created a hunger and thirst within my heart for a deeper relationship with You, as well as with the Father and with the Holy Spirit. Be pleased, Lord Jesus, to send Your Holy Spirit mightily upon me. I surrender myself totally to You. Forgive all my sins, and be pleased to baptize me with the Holy Spirit. Equip and empower me to magnify Your Name by advancing the gospel in the power of the Holy Spirit. Thank you. Amen.

(Pause, listening for additional guidance. Obey.)

What to Expect

Expect that Jesus heard your prayer, and that He will answer it in His time and in His way. Do not expect the same set of experiences that Jesus is giving to person kneeling next to you. Their hands might start to shake, or they may dissolve into tears, or bubble over with joy, or feel heat and see fire, or feel deeply loved. You may experience nothing at all. Many people experience a renewed hunger to read Scripture. Some people – but not all – begin to speak in tongues or prophecy. Others become very quiet. One man reported, "I felt like a rock; I did not feel anything at all. I went away disappointed." Much to his surprise, however, a few weeks later others told him that his preaching was clothed with a new sense of power and love. Nicki Gumbel experienced an electric shock of love; and Charles Finney, waves of liquid love. Some people experience a tangible manifestation initially, but in the days and weeks that follow, feel nothing at all.

Dr. R.A. Torrey noted that the primary evidence in Scripture of baptism with the Holy Spirit was new power for service.[73]

Jesus is not only very creative; He is also sensitive to our personalities and needs. To some, He whispers, and to others He thunders. Often, He deals with artists in one way and engineers in another. Our goal is not to have an over-the-top experience but to ask in obedient faith and leave the results to God. The Holy Spirit will work within us in personal ways because He Himself is a Person who is powerful and not merely an abstract force or influence.

---

[73] R.A. Torrey, *The Holy Spirit: Who He Is and What He Does*, 54.

Routine Maintenance ... which is anything but routine

Dr. Torrey continues:

> During the World's Fair in Chicago in 1893, Mr.
> Moody brought together, in Chicago, some of the most
> renowned and most able Bible teachers and Gospel
> preachers from all parts of the world. He said: "For
> years I have been going to the world; now the world is
> coming to me, and I am going to see that they get the
> Gospel through the best preachers in their different
> languages that I can secure." He brought famous men
> from England, Scotland, Ireland, France, Germany,
> Austria, Russia and other lands. Among others, he
> brought a man who had been wonderfully used in his
> own country. He took this man first to Northfield, and
> then brought him on to Chicago. When he was giving
> his first lecture in the lecture room of the Bible Institute
> in Chicago, Mr. Moody said to me: "I want you to hear
> this man and give me your opinion of him." So when
> the crowd had gathered we slipped into a back seat
> where we would not be seen. After listening for a while,
> Mr. Moody slipped out and beckoned me to follow. We
> went up to his office and sat down. Mr. Moody turned
> to me and said: "What do you think of him?" I replied:
> "I have nothing I wish to say." "Well," he said, "I have
> something I wish to say: I would give every penny it
> cost me to bring him to this country if he were back
> home again. He has lost his unction!"

Oh, it is an awful thing to lose one's unction! Mr.
Moody used to say that he would rather die than to lose
the power of the Holy Spirit in his work. But we
certainly shall lose our unction unless we seek a new

filling with the Spirit for each new emergency of Christian service.[74]

In order to maintain a posture of availability before God, I routinely follow a three-step process:

1. Palms down

As I turn my palms down, I examine my heart – or better, I invite Jesus to examine my heart. I drop all my sins at the foot of the cross.

2. Palms up

My prayer goes something like this:

> Lord Jesus, fill me afresh, anew with the Holy Spirit, and continue growing Your fruit in my life – Your love, joy, peace ….

3. Right hand raised toward heaven, left hand resting on my head

> "Lord Jesus, pour out Your Holy Spirit upon me. Baptize me anew and afresh and with Your blessed Holy Spirit. Equip and empower me for all the ministries You have for me today. Activate and release the spiritual gifts needed to advance Your agenda. (Then, I name gifts that come to mind such as teaching, healing, leadership, evangelism…) Thank you, Jesus. Amen."

Again I quote R.A. Torrey:

---

[74] R.A. Torrey, *The Holy Spirit: Who He Is and What He Does*, 39.

I am often asked if I have received "The Second Blessing." I certainly have, - and the third and the fourth and the fifth and the three hundredth, and the three hundred and fortieth, and I am looking for the three hundred and forty-first today. One of the commonest mistakes today, and one of the gravest, is that many people are trying to work today in the power of some baptism with the Spirit that they received a year ago, or two years ago, or five years ago, or ten years ago, as the case may be. Don't make that mistake. However definitely you may have been "baptized with the Holy Spirit" in the past you need, you must have, a new infilling for each new emergency of Christian service. And you must seek it in God's appointed way - by prayer (Luke 11: 13), definite prayer for a definite blessing.[75]

And so, dear coworkers,

- Cultivate a relationship with the Holy Spirit! and,
- Have the time of your life serving Jesus in the power of the Holy Spirit!

Come, Holy Spirit, come!

---

[75] R.A. Torrey, *The Holy Spirit: Who He Is and What He Does*, 39.

For Further Reflection

Chapter 12: Jesus, A Spirit-Empowered Man

1. Before reading this chapter, what answer would you have given to someone who asked, "Why was Jesus able to open blind eyes, cure lepers, and drive out evil spirits?"

2. What questions about this subject still linger in your mind?

3. What is your understanding of the implications of John 14:12 for us today:

   > *Truly, truly, I say to you, whoever believes in me will also do the works that I do; and <u>greater works</u> than these will he do, because I am going to the Father.* John 14:12, ESV

Chapter 13: Pentecost

1. Which parts of this chapter were helpful for you? In what way?

2. From your perspective, what are the strengths and weakness of the metaphor at the conclusion of this chapter?

Chapter 14: Baptism with the Holy Spirit: Real People, Real Stories

1. What conclusions can we draw from a side-by-side comparison of the stories included in this chapter?

2. What are the implications for you? And for us?

3. "Baptism with the Holy Spirit" - What is your story?

Chapter 15: Your Personal Pentecost: Preparing for and Receiving Empowerment

1. Have you come to the point in your life where you would like someone to lay hands on you and join with you in inviting Jesus to baptize you with the Holy Spirit?

2. If yes, who can you ask? When will you ask them? What do you expect will happen?

3. While you wait for your prayer appointment, what steps will you take to prepare yourself to receive all that Jesus has for you?

PART V: LIVING EMPOWERED

Understanding the empowering dimension of the Holy Spirit's work is good. Living empowered is better by far.

Chapter 17: When Our Candle Becomes a Torch

For most of us most of the time life is very ordinary. We exercise, eat, sleep, spend time with our family and friends, weed the garden, check our social networks, work, and volunteer in our community and church. But once in a while the Holy Spirit comes "upon" us and momentarily lifts us to a whole new level of engagement, empowering us to cooperate with Jesus to accomplish something that He wants done.

In November, 2012, Cindy sent an email inviting me to serve as the lead teacher for a conference in Holland, Michigan, entitled "Growing the Church in the Power of the Holy Spirit."[76] Initially, I felt both honored and inadequate. "I'm just a normal person," I thought,"Can't they find someone with more

---

[76] Zeb Bradford Long, Paul Stokes, and Cindy Strickler, *Growing the Church in the Power of the Holy Spirit* (Grand Rapids: Zondervan, 2009).

experience and better credentials?!?" After praying over the invitation for a few weeks and discussing it with my wife and a few intercessors, I sensed a green light to say "Yes" … and then the hard work of prayer and preparation began in earnest.

On March 8, 2013, two days before I boarded the plane to travel to Michigan, I recorded some of the guidance I had been receiving from the Lord for our time together at the conference.

> A. Yesterday while reading in Mark 1:2-3, ESV, *prepare the way of the Lord,* I had the sense that one of our primary responsibilities as a leadership team would be to cooperate with the Holy Spirit to prepare the way for the Lord to minister among us. His work is second to none.

> B. I was also reading in 1 Timothy 4:14, ESV:

>> *Do not neglect the gift you have, which was given you by prophecy when the council of elders laid their hands on you.*

> My sense is that we are to offer appointments with "prophetic prayer teams." The primary need will not be for inner healing of life's messes but for prophetic prayer teams to speak words of encouragement and guidance into the lives of others.

> C. This morning I read about Jesus' baptism (Mark 1:9-11). Jesus <u>saw</u> *the heavens being torn open and the Spirit descending on Him like a dove,* (1:10, ESV). I am asking Jesus to give me eyes to see what He is doing in the spiritual realm in my life and especially in the lives of others and in the group. Jesus also <u>heard</u> *a voice come from heaven,* (1:11, ESV), and I am asking Jesus for ears to hear what He is saying to me and to us.

On the opening day of the conference (Monday), my first two talks unfolded as planned. However, the evening session tested my resolve to participate in the "dance of cooperation" with the Father, Son, and Holy Spirit. When it was all over and I was once again alone in my room, I recorded the following:

March 10, 2013
Holland, Michigan

A few hours ago I completed my third speaking assignment for today. Prior to speaking, while conference participants were joyfully engaged in worship, I was having a perfectly miserable time on the sidelines wrestling with what I sensed Jesus was nudging me to say and do during the evening session. During worship I pulled Jennifer aside and asked her to pray for me. Terri also sensed my anxiety, rested a hand on my shoulder, and quietly prayed for me.

Eventually my time to speak came and Jesus enabled me to obey His guidance and dance with Him. That's the metaphor we are using for staying in step with the Spirit – the "dance of cooperation'.

In the end I felt drained, energized, and deeply happy. When I finally returned to my room for the night I opened my Bible and read, *Blessed are those who hear the word of God and obey it,* Luke 11:28, NRSV. I felt blessed! Jesus opened my ears to receive guidance and Jesus gave me the courage to obey.

So, what happened?

Normally when I teach I rely on my carefully crafted notes and power points. However, the guidance Jesus gave me was to set them all aside and simply tell the group that Jesus Christ loves His Bride, the Church. That's it – one sentence. The president of a seminary was in the audience and all Jesus gave me to say was one sentence.

When I stood before the group to speak, the Lord downloaded a great introduction. "While you were all having a great time singing about stepping into the river with Jesus," I said, "I was having a perfectly miserable time on the sidelines wrestling with what I sensed Jesus was prompting me to say to you tonight." Then, I shared the sentence, and as I did the Spirit fell upon me and I could barely speak. After a few moments Jesus helped me to compose myself and He downloaded the next thing I needed to say … and the next … and the next. Many of the key points from my carefully prepared talk were included but in a slightly different – and more effective – order. After speaking for about 20 minutes the Lord gave me a wonderful conclusion and I sat down.

Jennifer and Deanna rushed forward filled with joy and affirmation. "The Lord lifted you to a whole new level! You were a changed man!" Tears welled up as I protested, "But I really felt out of my comfort zone." Their response: "You never looked so natural."

Truly, blessed are those who hear the word of God and obey it.

On Wednesday, the Lord brought to fruition His pre-conference guidance regarding prophetic prayer ministry.

Journal Entry, Wednesday evening, March 13, 2013

Prior to the conference (i.e., on March 8), the Lord planted in my mind the thought that, while at the conference in Holland on "Growing the Church in the Power of the Holy Spirit," we were to offer opportunities for participants to receive prayer from Prophetic Prayer Ministry Teams. I "tested" the idea by sharing it with the leadership team and their responses were very positive.

At many PRMI events we offer an opportunity for people to receive "Healing Prayer" or "Soaking Prayer"– precious times to receive healing from Jesus through Prayer Teams that are working in cooperation with the Holy Spirit to bring healing to inner wounds. Generally, the individuals who sign up for one of these thirty-minute appointments are saying, "An aspect of my life is a mess and I need help." However, Prophetic Prayer Ministry would be different. The person who signs up for a fifteen-minute appointment is saying, "I need to hear a word from the Lord for my life!"

On Wednesday morning of the Conference, while my attention was focused on other things, the thought suddenly came that "now is the time" to organize the Prophetic Prayer Teams and have them ready to go following lunch. After double-checking with Tom and Mary, I alerted Sheri, Terri, and Gina, and they immediately went to work behind the scenes to select people with prophetic gifts and to put them into teams. People who have prophetic gifts love this type of ministry! They feel like kids turned loose in a candy store.

Just before dismissing for lunch I presented the opportunity to the group and invited people to sign up.

I reminded everyone that "one word from the Lord is better than 1000 elsewhere." We encouraged people to sign up as individuals, couples, or ministry coworkers.

Within minutes most of the 48 slots were filled!

People are hungry to hear a word from the Lord!

When the conference was over, I boarded a plane and headed toward home. Due to delays, I missed my connection and spent the night in Chicago's O'Hare airport – not my first choice by a long shot but it gave me ample opportunity for further reflection as well as time to document the amazing work that the Holy Spirit had done among us on the final day of the conference. Approximately 150 people – mainly CRC and RCA church leaders – were in attendance and Jesus had us dancing together with Him. Here's what I wrote:

> Many of us believe that on Thursday, March 14, 2013, a tectonic shift occurred in the spiritual realm pertaining to the advance of the gospel and growth of the church in West Michigan. The gates are now open wide for the King of glory to come in.

> Although accurate, words like "remarkable" and "amazing" only begin to describe our sense of what God did through the men and women gathered for this spiritually historic event.

> In the course of the morning God worked through Dave and his anointed teaching on "*kairos* moments" to build our faith. I followed Dave by teaching briefly on obstacles to the dance of cooperation with the Father, Son, and Holy Spirit … and then we began to dance.

I concluded my teaching by shifting our attention from theoretical obstacles that the church might experience to obstacles that we were experiencing in West Michigan.

I began by reading from Isaiah 40. Backup a step. As noted above, on March 8, my regular Bible reading included John the Baptist's admonishment in Mark 1:3 to *prepare the way for the Lord.* While at the conference that phrase kept going through my mind. After sharing that with the group I proclaimed,

> *A voice is calling,*
> *"Clear the way for the Lord in the wilderness;*
> *Make smooth in the desert a highway for our*
> *God....*
> *Then the glory of the Lord will be revealed,*
> *And all flesh will see it together;*
> *For the mouth of the Lord has spoken."*
> Isaiah 40:3-5, ESV

After reading Isaiah's words to the group, I summarized by saying, "This is a prophetic word for us – here, now, today."

I handed the mic to Mary who described the remarkable move of God that occurred in Michigan in the 1970s, but was shut down by the clergy.[77]

Tim followed by talking about the power of "identificational repentance" to pull down strongholds, break the enemy's foothold, and open closed doors.

---

[77] Interestingly, God's work in Michigan in the early 1970s dovetailed with a revival that broke out on the campus of Wheaton College near Chicago.

Next, I began to implement the first "picture" that the Holy Spirit had put in my mind a few days earlier – a picture that did not make sense to me until that very moment – a picture of the group in two circles. Suddenly the Holy Spirit revealed to me that we as a group were supposed to do what He had shown me. I asked the group to get up out of their chairs and form two circles:

1. A large circle around the perimeter of the room.

2. A smaller circle of 10-15 pastors in the center of the room with chairs facing outward. The guidance for the pastors in the center circle to face outward did not come until the instant we began to move in obedience.

Once in circles we invited Ruth to share an illustration from her missionary work among Muslims about the power of forgiveness to pave the way for the gospel's advance. As Ruth was speaking I received guidance to begin the process of identificational repentance by inviting the pastors to look at the people surrounding them and complete the sentence: "Please forgive us for …."

Following a series of confessions I instructed the people to respond by declaring in unison, "In the name of Jesus Christ we forgive you."

Next, I invited the people to address the pastors and finish the sentence, "Please forgive us for …."

Guidance came that after the pastors stood and declared in unison, "In the name of Jesus Christ we forgive you," the pastors were, in Korean style, to pronounce blessings over the people.

Then, the Lord instructed me to declare, "Based on the authority entrusted to me as a servant of Jesus Christ, I declare that the chains are broken and that the obstacles hindering the advance of the gospel in our areas are removed!" The ring of authority in my voice as these words thundered forth surprised even me.

In situations like this we must not only renounce and turn from; we must also announce and turn to. "Binding" is to be followed by "loosing." After old clothes have been removed, new clothes must be put on. We do this by making announcements to the spiritual realm, declaring truth. Tim wisely picked up the mic at this juncture and declared to the powers of darkness in the heavenly realms that "Jesus Christ reigns here. We are under His Lordship."

To implement a second picture that the Lord had given to me a few days earlier, I asked eight volunteers to come up front, each representing a decade, starting with the 60s. A pregnant sister and her husband volunteered to stand at the end of the line and represent future generations. I invited the audience to extend their hands toward these representatives and, as each took a step forward, pronounce blessings over the generation they represented. As this was happening –and it was glorious – I "saw" a sparkling river of life flowing from generation to generation and into the future.

At this point in our wonderful dance the Spirit fell upon Mary and she had a vision. She took the mic and described to the group that Jesus opened her eyes to see a portal to heaven opened over us and a great cloud of witnesses cheering us on. She sensed Dr. Victor Matthews was there, and her godly father, Rev. John

Morren, supporting us, and that the prayers of the saints of generations past were the foundation for what was happening among us at that moment. Others had visions of their aunts, uncles, parents, and grandparents standing together in heaven watching and cheering us on.

The thought came to me that we needed to sing. After all, true worship is also warfare. I said to the group, "We need to sing. Is a song going though anyone's mind?" Immediately a lady called out, "O God Our Help in Ages Past." We followed that song with others including "Spirit of the Living God, Fall Afresh On Me," and "Praise God From Whom All Blessing Flow." Then, we broke for lunch.

Did anyone take a picture of this beautiful and triumphant dance? Not to my knowledge. But its power, beauty, and majesty are recorded on heaven's Facebook page ... and in our hearts. We will never be the same. Nor will His Bride in West Michigan.

As the dance glided toward a close, Jesus whispered to my inner man, "I'm lifting you to a new level of leadership."

Is every day as powerful and dynamic as those four days in Holland, Michigan? No. Most days are ordinary, very ordinary. However, when Jesus determines to do a special work through us, and when we determine to cooperate with Him, for that moment in time the Holy Spirit empowers us and our candle becomes a torch.[78] Glory!

---

[78] This analogy is rooted in Gideon's experience with the Holy Spirit. See Judges 6-8, and the chapter in this book entitled, "The Spirit Empowered Gideon."

Chapter 18: Receiving Guidance

As the leadership team at a Dunamis Fellowship event waited quietly in prayer prior to the evening session, I "heard" the word "holy." How did I hear it? I am not sure but I know that I know that the Holy Spirit imbedded the word "holy" on my heart. No one on the leadership team had been talking about holiness. The word was not in our notes. Yet, quietly and distinctly it came to mind. However, I refrained from saying to the group, "I'm hearing the word 'holy.'" Why? Perhaps because the impression caught me by surprise. Perhaps because at that moment my confidence level in God's willingness to speak to me, and in my capacity to receive guidance from Jesus through the Holy Spirit, was relatively low. Doubts lingered.

While I was still processing and analyzing what I had "heard," the team meeting concluded and we moved to the chapel for our evening session. When the worship team began, guess what their theme was: holiness.

In retrospect, I believe that if I had voiced what I heard, the worship team could have led with even greater confidence knowing that they, and we, were in alignment with God's heart for that evening.

God used this experience to build my confidence level. I walked away saying to myself, "Yes, Phil, Jesus speaks to you, too. When you listen, you, too, can receive guidance from Him through the Holy Spirit."

And so can you.

Even a casual reading of the Old and New Testaments draws our attention to the many times and variety of ways that the Holy Spirit guides His people. After all, Jesus Himself declared that one of the Holy Spirit's responsibilities is to give guidance, and to do so in such a manner that points our attention to Jesus.

> *When the Spirit of truth comes, <u>he will guide you</u> into all the truth, for he will not speak on his own authority, but whatever he hears he will speak, and he will declare to you the things that are to come. He will glorify me [Jesus], for he will take what is mine and declare it to you.* John 16:13-14, ESV

Jesus is willing to speak to us and He has given us, as Christians, the capacity to hear His voice.

> *He said, "<u>My sheep hear my voice</u>, and I know them, and they follow me."* John 10:27, ESV

> *See that you do not refuse him who is speaking.* Hebrews 12:25, ESV

How the Holy Spirit Guides Us

1. Guidance through Scripture

A year after Teri and I began our first full-time ministry position in Evansville, Indiana, in 1975, someone blessed us with $3000 to use as a down payment for a house. (Yes, that was sufficient.) After house-hunting for several months we found one that met our criteria. Before submitting a formal offer we decided to think and pray about that option for one more day. The next morning, during my regular Bible reading, the Holy Spirit highlighted this phrase in my mind and heart: *You enlarge my steps under me,* Psalm 18:36, NAS. Following a brief debate with myself, I decided to take this as guidance that the Lord had a bigger place for us. Sure enough, a week later, a much better home came on the market and we purchased it.

Another experience of guidance through Scripture occurred following a teaching on the baptism with the Holy Spirit at a Dunamis event. My prayer partner and I prayed for several people but we did not see any obvious manifestations of the Spirit's presence, which, honestly, was a little disappointing for me. I discussed this with the Lord, who focused my attention on Paul's words in 2 Corinthians 5:7, *We walk by faith, not by sight.* Whereas I wanted to see results, God used Scripture to communicate to me that He wanted us to believe that He was working even when we did not see the evidence.

2. Guidance through prophetic words

The Bible contains numerous examples of God guiding people through prophetic words.

An example from the Old Testament:

> *When Rehoboam came to Jerusalem, he assembled all the house of Judah and the tribe of Benjamin, 180,000 chosen warriors to fight against the house of Israel, to restore the kingdom to Rehoboam the son of Solomon. 22 But the word of God came to Shemaiah the man of God: 23 "Say to Rehoboam the son of Solomon, king of Judah, and to all the house of Judah and Benjamin, and to the rest of the people, 24 'Thus says the Lord, You shall not go up or fight against your relatives the people of Israel. Every man return to his home, for this thing is from me.'" So they listened to the word of the Lord and went home again, according to the word of the Lord.* 1 Kings 12:21-24, ESV

An example from the New Testament:

> *They [the chief priests and scribes] told him [King Herod], "In Bethlehem of Judea, for so it is written by the prophet: 'And you, O Bethlehem, in the land of Judah, are by no means least among the rulers of Judah; for from you shall come a ruler who will shepherd my people Israel.'"* Matthew 2:5-6, ESV

A personal example:

The Lord used a prophetic word spoken through Julie to alert me that He was preparing future ministry assignments for me and preparing me for them. During the course of a group prayer time, the Lord led her to speak prophetically to me saying, "The Lord is writing appointments in your schedule book," and "The Lord is giving you a size-bigger coat" [referring, I believe, to an increase in spiritual authority and power].

Very encouraging and affirming.

3. Guidance through dreams and visions

Generally, dreams occur at night and visions during the day. These methods of guidance are relatively common in both the Old Testament and the New.

Examples from the Old Testament:

- God used Joseph to interpret Pharaoh's dream thereby giving guidance for Egypt's future. Genesis 41:28-30

- God spoke to Solomon in a dream. 1 Kings 3:4-15

Examples from the New Testament:

- *There was a disciple at Damascus named Ananias. The Lord said to him in a vision, "Ananias." And he said, "Here I am, Lord." 11 And the Lord said to him, "Rise and go to the street called Straight, and at the house of Judas look for a man of Tarsus named Saul, for behold, he is praying, 12 and he has seen in a vision a man named Ananias come in and lay his hands on him so that he might regain his sight."* Acts 9:10-12, ESV

- *But as he considered these things, behold, an angel of the Lord appeared to him in a dream, saying, "Joseph, son of David, do not fear to take Mary as your wife, for that which is conceived in her is from the Holy Spirit.* Matthew 1:20, ESV

- God gave guidance to Peter through a vision. Acts 10:9-17

- God combined a vision with the Holy Spirit's voice in Acts 10:19-20, ESV

    And while Peter was pondering the <u>vision</u>, the Spirit said to him, "Behold, three men are looking for you. 20 Rise and go down and accompany them without hesitation, for I have sent them."

- *A <u>vision</u> appeared to Paul in the night: a man of Macedonia was standing there, urging him and saying, "Come over to Macedonia and help us." And when Paul had seen the <u>vision</u>, immediately we sought to go on into Macedonia, concluding that God had called us to preach the gospel to them.* Acts 16:9-10, ESV

In May, 2002, I noted in my journal that "More and more while engaged in prayer ministry the Lord is giving me pictures of something he wants communicated. The frequency with which they come both surprises and delights me."

In recent years, God has used a specific type of dream – I call it a "snake dream" – to warn me about heightened spiritual warfare. Here's an example from my journal:

> I spent part of last night (Thursday, September 13, 2007) caught up in a vivid dream battling demonic powers. Two snakes, one large, the other smaller, appeared. I kept trying to wrestle them down, to hold them down. They kept trying to bite me. Finally I put them in a cage that had a clear material like Plexiglas on the front of it. People (adults and kids) came by and teased the snakes. They, in turn, struck against the Plexiglas again and again causing it to bulge out. I watched fearing that it would break. I went for help,

looking for a way to kill the snakes. I returned to find that the snakes had broken the Plexiglas and were slithering away. I grabbed them and held them and yelled for Teri to go to the hardware store and get a hatchet. She went but took a long time. While she was gone, I grew weary and threw the small snake into the freezer. I thought, "Now I only have one to deal with. Soon Teri will be back and we will kill them both." But after I walked away, someone opened the freezer door … and got bit.

Eventually someone came from the store with a big machete. I went to kill the snake in the freezer only to see the door open and a man limping away. He had many bandages on his side and arm because he had opened the door and had been bitten repeatedly. Thank God he was still alive but the snake had escaped.

I woke up and prayed protection (the blood of Jesus) over myself, the room, and my family. Immediately I had a sense that I was to write down the dream. I did.

During the dream I did not feel fear. After the dream I felt anger because I realized that when the snakes could not get me, they struck another man while I was gone.

Beware! Be vigilant! There are at least two snakes still on the loose.

Footnote: Three days later we learned the identity of the man who got bit. We learned that someone close to us was having an affair.

As I noted earlier, in November, 2012, Cindy asked me to pray about serving as the lead teacher for the PRMI conference

166

entitled "Growing the Church in the Power of the Holy Spirit." After a season of prayer, I said "Yes." The picture that came to mind as I contemplated what I was being asked to do was this: I saw a pair of shoes that were big, really big. When I stepped into them, my little feet did not even come close to filling them.

I sent an email to Jennifer, one of our intercessors, saying, "Join me in asking Jesus to grow my feet to fill these shoes."

God did show up in remarkable ways as detailed in the earlier chapter entitled, "When Our Candle Becomes a Torch."

On another occasion, I recorded the following:

> Yesterday Julia and Andrew invited several people to their home to say "farewell" to Angie, who was moving with her family to Australia. Angie is a dynamic, high-level prophetic, intercessor – a "seer" who has worked very effectively to evangelize others. As the group gathered around Angie to pray, I "saw" the mantle of Elijah being passed to Elisha. After the time of prayer, Angie came directly to me (she said later that the Lord directed her to me) and I shared this impression. She, in turn, responded with surprise, awe, and delight, and reported that several years earlier the Lord had given her a vision concerning Elijah and Elisha. Further, that very morning the Lord brought the vision back to mind and she asked Him for confirmation. The Lord's word through me came as confirmation. She looked intently at me and said with a hint of amazement and wonder, "You can hear God!"

As an interesting aside, earlier in that week Teri asked me if we needed to attend that dinner for Angie – we already had so many other things on our schedule. I responded with a firm, "Yes." Now I know why.

4. Guidance through an "audible" impression

In November, 2003, following a Dunamis event, I wrote:

> I just returned from the conference, "Gateways to Empowered Ministry" where I helped with leadership, teaching, and prayer ministries. Early in the flow of the conference I "heard" Jesus whisper to my heart that He was going to teach me to teach and communicate. Throughout the event, I sensed the Spirit prompting me in other ways, too, but His voice was so quiet – like a whisper on the wind. I found myself saying, "Lord, can't You talk a little louder? Or, can't You at least repeat what You just said? It's so faint!" Later, during a debriefing session, Jon DeBruyn reflected that "God often speaks in a wisp; that is, half a whisper."

One of the many examples in Scripture where God guided people through audible impressions occurred in Acts 8:

> *Now an angel of the Lord <u>said</u> to Philip, "Rise and go toward the south to the road that goes down from Jerusalem to Gaza." This is a desert place. ... And the Spirit <u>said</u> to Philip, "Go over and join this chariot."* Acts 8:26, 29, ESV

Likewise, many times in the Old Testament we read, *The word of the Lord came to ....* Frequently, when I come across that phrase during the course of my regular Bible reading, I pause and pray, "Jesus, let Your word come to me with greater frequency and clarity."

A lapse of time may occur between God's word and its fulfillment. In 2001, while cross-country skiing on the Vasa Trail in Traverse City, Michigan, and praying about our future, I distinctly "heard" the Holy Spirit whisper to my heart, "I'm preparing a place for you." A few days later, I asked Teri what the Lord had been saying to her recently. She commented that while she was attending a service for Lent a few days earlier and praying about our future, the Lord impressed on her the phrase, "I'm preparing a place for you."

Four years later, Jesus brought us to that place.

Audible impressions are often very quiet and hence, easily missed. We hear but we doubt. Once, when four of us were praying with a lady who was experiencing eye problems, I sensed the Holy Spirit directing me to say to her, "In the name of Jesus Christ, you are healed." I hesitated, analyzing my options. Because I did not have the courage to step out in faith and say it, I went home wondering what would have happened if I had simply obeyed. The worst that would have happened was nothing at all – which might bruise my ego but otherwise do no harm.

While preparing to teach a Bible study on James 3:1, I kept getting the impression that I was to call someone into the teaching ministry. I began the class by saying, "This isn't my normal style of operation, but I sense that I am supposed to say to you that God wants to call someone in our midst into a teaching ministry." As soon as the class ended, Pete came forward and said, "Can we talk?" He proceeded to tell me that this was the second time that he (a new believer) had sensed God was speaking to him. Time will tell what God has in store for Pete.

Sometimes the Holy Spirit's leadership through audible impressions is very direct. In May, 2003, I was scheduled to teach at a Dunamis event on "The Holy Spirit and Evangelism." As we prepared for the morning session, the Lord whispered to me that we, as a group, needed to hear Scripture read out loud. "What text?" I asked. The answer that came to mind was the verses in Joshua 3 and 4 regarding memorial stones. In addition, the Lord indicated that Andrew was to read it. A short time later (still prior to the start of the meeting), the Lord put two words in my mind: "process" and "digest." As the worship began, I kept praying about how to proceed. A moment later, it was time for me to step to the microphone. Rather than launching into the teaching assignment that was on the schedule, I reminded the group of the value of hearing God's Word, and invited Andrew to read Joshua 3 and 4. He did. Following that I shared that I sensed a need for us to digest and process all that we had been learning. After instructing participants to get into small groups, I watched as conversations flowed and spontaneous prayer times unfolded within various groups. As this was progressing, the Lord impressed on me that there was one more step. He gave me the words "thirsts" and "desires." Eventually, I invited people to remain in groups and share thirsts and desires (longings) that continued to linger in their hearts. More intense sharing occurred. As they were sharing with one another, the Lord impressed on me that the work He wanted to do in individuals during the morning session was done and that I was not to teach. Hence, I ended the time with a prayer of gratitude and turned the mic over to Jon.

Later that day, several people came to me and commented on how meaningful that morning session had been for them.

One of the lessons I am learning is to say what God says without adding to it or revising it. While praying for Eric, the Lord clearly put in my mind the phrase, "I saw the heavens opened." Rather than simply stating that phrase, I paraphrased it; and in so doing, I believe it lost its power. In retrospect, I believe that I should have simply said, "Eric, I'm hearing the phrase, 'I saw the heavens opened,'" and trusted that if more were to be said, Jesus would give it to me or to one of the other prayer team members.

Incidentally, during that prayer time for Eric, my right hand began to tremble and I had the sense that God's power was flowing through that hand. However, I did not place that hand directly on his head ... and I believe that I should have.

In September, 2007, I served on a prayer team at a conference in Traverse City, Michigan, sponsored by the ministry that Francis and Judith MacNutt led (Christian Healing Ministries, www.christianhealingmin.org), entitled "Leaders in Healing Ministry." Conference participants who desired to receive prayer made 30-minute appointments with a prayer team.

During the course of the week, I participated in eleven 30-minute sessions. What a joy! I stand amazed at Jesus' creativity, compassion, and power. Here is one example:

Generally, my prayer partner and I began the session by asking, "What would you like Jesus to do for you?" After three to five minutes of conversation, we moved into a time of prayer by inviting Jesus and the Holy Spirit to manifest His presence in our midst. Then, we paused for a time of silence to listen for the Spirit's guidance. As guidance came, we proceeded in prayer.

An elderly man with a walking stick – which he placed on the shelf behind us – came for prayer. After a few minutes of conversation, we paused to invite Jesus to draw near. As we waited in silence, I heard the word "Father." I thought, "'Father;' what am I supposed to do with that?" I stood, moved behind the man, placed my hands on his shoulders, and said, "I'm hearing the word 'father.'" I paused, and more words began to flow – beautiful words of encouragement pertaining to him serving as a father to people in his family and church. A few minutes later, a crazy idea entered my mind. "Take his walking stick and 'knight' him." "This is weird," I thought, but I walked to the front of him, picked up his walking stick from the shelf, placed one end on his shoulder, and said, "Please look at me. I believe I am to knight you for your new calling." I did, expressing words of commissioning and blessing as the Lord put them on my heart.

When the session was over, the man's face radiated new life. He looked ten years younger and twenty pounds lighter. When I saw him the next morning, his countenance continued to reflect refreshment and joy.

On another occasion, when I landed in Traverse City, Michigan, on Wednesday evening, September 25, 2013, to participate on the leadership team for the Dunamis Conference on "The Healing Ministry of Jesus," I was greeted by Kate and Mark. Kate gave me a big hug, along with two-dozen beautiful, yellow roses. My first thought was, "I'm a guy. What am I to do with these?" I decided to take them to the site where we were meeting. "Here, put these in water," I said to Anita. "Let's enjoy them throughout the conference."

Brigitte Anne, a Christ-centered, Holy Spirit-empowered young lady who is in her late 20s, served on our intercession team. On one occasion we as a group set aside time to minister to her. As she sat in the center of the circle, the entire group gathered around to bless her in Jesus' name. I stood on the outside of the group, interceding. Out of the blue, the Holy Spirit whispered to me, "Address her as if you are her earthly father, and tell her that you are sorry for abandoning her." The Spirit's whisper caught me by surprise and I wrestled with it. "Lord, is this from you?? And, if it is, is that all you want me to say??" The thought came to me, "Just speak the words I

172

have given you and more will come." With hesitant steps, I
moved around the circle to a point where I could see Brigitte
Anne's face. Eventually, Deanna, who headed our prayer team,
noticed me and motioned for me to step forward. I approached
Brigitte, kneeled directly in front of her, put my hand on her
knee, looked her full in the face, and said with an emotion-
filled voice – the Holy Spirit was upon me and I could hardly
speak – "Brigitte Anne, I want to address you as your earthly
father. I am sorry for abandoning you. Please forgive me. I
love you. I am proud of you and pleased with the woman you
are becoming. Your feet are on a firm foundation."

A big smile graced her beautiful face, along with tears. Many
others in the group were also in tears.

Later, during a debriefing, I learned that Brigitte Anne had
been abandoned by three fathers. She also said, "When you
looked at me, I wanted to say, 'I love you!' … but I think you
are a married man!" As we all laughed, I affirmed, "Yes, I am a
married man … but I'm old enough to be your father. You may
tell me you love me anytime!"

At the end of the conference, several people, including Brigitte,
stayed to help clean up. "Who will take the roses home?"
someone asked. Eyes turned toward Brigitte and she received
them with great joy. "These are from my daddy," she said with
delight.

I feel like I have a new daughter.

After leaving the conference, I headed back across town and
stopped at Kate's house. As I told her about Brigitte Anne and
the yellow roses, she wept with deep joy.

Who but God could create such a beautiful arrangement?!?

5. Guidance through circumstances

Just as a barometer is a helpful but unreliable indicator of tomorrow's weather, so circumstances alone are a helpful but unreliable indicator of God's will. In 1 Samuel 24:4, for example, circumstances aligned for David to kill Saul, but doing so would have been wrong. On the other hand, Gideon's experience with the fleece (Judges 6:36-40) proved to be a very reliable indicator of God's will for him at that time. If we must choose between circumstances and God's Word, the right choice is to follow God's Word and trust Him to iron-out circumstances.

Nevertheless, wise people pay attention to circumstances. Generally, when God opens closed doors we go forward, and when He shuts doors, we hold back.

While in the Holy Land, on Saturday evening, November 16, 2013, several people from our group sat in a circle near the shore of the Sea of Galilee, and listened as Andrew shared about his love for Israel. Following his talk, with the sound of the waves in the background, we broke into small groups for prayer. As Andrew, Sheryl, and others prayed for me, the Lord gave Sheryl a vision of a huge dam breaking [a dam big dam!], and water being released into a controlled channel.

I went to bed and woke up in the night with a song going through my mind – "I Have Made You a Watchman on the Wall" – a song Sheryl had sung at previous prayer gatherings. It is not unusual for a song to play in my mind, but I suddenly realized, "Hey! This is Jesus speaking to me! He is calling me to serve as a watchman on the wall!" (see Isaiah 62). That realization was followed by an intense burst of speaking in tongues that lasted for perhaps 10 seconds. Something nudged me to check the time. It was 4:27. Significance? Our room

number was 427! – a clear confirmation that this call, this
assignment, was for me.

6. Guidance through an inner peace

- *Let the <u>peace of Christ</u> rule in your hearts, to which
  indeed you were called in one body. And be thankful.*
  Colossians 3:15, ESV

- *The <u>peace of God</u>, which surpasses all understanding,
  will guard your hearts and your minds in Christ Jesus.*
  Philippians 4:7, ESV

While on a conference call with a ministry team for an event
that we were planning, I said, "Why don't we switch sessions
three and four?" After a brief pause, one of the ladies replied,
"I have 'check' in my spirit regarding that. I think we should
leave it the way it is."

Oswald Chambers observed, "If we are going to choose what
he does NOT want, He will check [as a rider pulls gently on the
horse's reigns] and we must heed.[79]

The phrase "check in my spirit" is another way of saying, "I
lack peace about that;" or "When I consider that, I feel
unsettled." When we are seeking to live in a way that pleases
God, He will guide us through the presence or absence of
peace. Pay attention to your "gut;" yet, realize that it might be
wrong. In the next chapter, we will say more about how to
discern if an impression or a word is truly from God, or not.

7. Guidance through an inner "knowing"

---

[79] Oswald Chambers, *My Utmost for His Highest*, n.d., reading for June 3.

Catherine Marshall wrote,

> One evening my husband Peter and I had planned to see
> a particular movie. It turned out to be a disappointing
> evening in every way. Long queues made it impossible
> even to get near the theatre. Then a store which we
> thought we might visit proved to be closed.
>
> On the way home, having been frustrated at every turn,
> Peter and I compared notes and found that earlier, each
> of us had had a strong inner feeling that we should not
> go. But neither had verbalized this, fearing to
> disappoint the other, especially since there was not
> reason to give except the inner direction.[80]

The well-known author Agnes Sanford related a similar
experience. She had an important engagement in Richmond,
Virginia.

> Several hours previous to departure time, however,
> Agnes was aware of a strong 'stop' from the Spirit.
> Since her mission was the Lord's work and she could
> see no reason for such guidance, she disregarded it and
> started. Before the train reached Richmond, there was a
> wreck on the track ahead. The train stopped in time, but
> the passengers were forced to sit up all night as they
> waited for the track to be cleared. "Afterward," Agnes
> said, "I realized that the inner Voice had been trying to
> warn me of this."[81]

In October, 2013, Jesus spoke to me through an email that I
received from Bishop Martin Odi in Uganda:

---

[80] Catherine Marshall, *The Helper* (Avon Books, 1978), 75-76.
[81] Catherin Marshall, 75-76.

> Philip, I kindly ask you to consider coming to give a lecture on the Holy Spirit to African Pastors. You will have new life in return!

As I read these words, the Holy Spirit quickened my spirit and I sensed that this was a "Macedonian call." In January, 2014, Bishop Odi sent a follow-up note:

> Philip, I wonder if it will be ok for you to prepare a full course in the Holy Spirit and you give lectures to my students in May when you come. It will require 6 hours of lecture each day for 4 days. We will also give a test after all lectures are done. There will be 25 or more students in all, and they are all pastors and overseers of churches in my region.

After praying about this and conferring with Teri, Sharon, and Jami, I said, "Yes."

If the voice within us is from the Holy Spirit, it will never suggest that we do something shady, dishonest, impure, unloving, or selfish. Nor will it ever tell us to do something contrary to Scripture. The Holy Spirit will always lead us in ways that harmonize with Scripture, point us toward Jesus, build up the Body, and advance the gospel.

8. Guidance through conscience

A conscience that is cleansed by the blood of Jesus (Hebrews 9:14) and quickened by the Holy Spirit serves as a reliable rudder for the ship of life.

When we arrived at the Chinese Community Church, it was part of a liberal denomination composed of congregationallygoverned churches. Hence, the denomination could make suggestions to local churches but could not issue mandates. As time progressed, it became apparent that the denomination was becoming even more liberal in three core areas: the authority of Scripture, the path to salvation, and the definition of marriage. For some people in the congregation, the denomination's choices mattered very little because as a local church we were free to set our own standards. For others, however, our link with the denomination became a matter of conscience. They viewed our relationship with the denomination as "guilt by association" and morally wrong. Their conflicted consciences would not let us as a congregation rest until we wrestled together with the issues, and voted to sever our ties with the denomination.

9. Guidance through men and women who are in leadership roles in the church

In November, 2009, while serving on the leadership team at a Dunamis Conference in Seattle at Tukwila Presbyterian Church, Pastor Nick pulled me aside and said, "We are hearing 'forgive one another' and 'love one another.' We think someone needs to teach from Ephesians 4:32-5:2, and we think you're the man. Will you do it?"

"Yes."

I went into a side room and asked God for guidance. A few minutes later the Lord downloaded a brief teaching (honest – He downloaded it). Normally it takes me a couple hours – or more – to prepare for a teaching of this nature. The heart and structure of this talk, along with an excellent visual illustration, came to me within about five minutes.

God helped me speak – a teaching that lasted around 15 minutes.

When I ended the teaching, I sensed the Lord nudging me to pray for the group. However, my mind was programmed to go with the schedule. Hence, I turned the microphone over to Steve to lead us into worship, and I stepped to the side of the room. For a few minutes, we as a group floundered, unsure of what to do next. Finally, I stepped over to Nick and Sandy and said, "I blew it; I think I was supposed to pray for the group." They said, "Do it now." I moved to the microphone. In response to the Lord's prompting, Sandy stood behind me with her hand resting lightly on my back, praying in tongues [very helpful!], and the Lord brought forth His prayer for His children. Next, Pastor Nick gave an invitation for people, who had some stuff they needed to let go of, to come to the altar and pray. And people came.

Throughout the remainder of the conference, reports kept trickling in about how significant that teaching and invitation was for people. To God be the glory!

Since He is very creative and resourceful, the Good Shepherd guides us through other means also; including, but not limited to:

- Guidance Through Christian Counselors (Proverbs 11:14)
- Guidance Through Logic and Common Sense (Acts 15:28-29)
- Guidance Through Signs (Judges 6:36-40; 2 Kings 20:8-11; 1 Samuel 10:1-13; Isaiah 7:11-14; Luke 2:1f.; John 20:30-31)
- Guidance Through Angels (Matthew 1:20; Acts 10:3-8, 30-32)

Live, Learn, and Move On

No one gets it right every time! Hence, give yourself much
grace. If we focus on our failures, the devil wins the day.
Accept God's forgiveness[82] and step back onto the dance floor.

Need Guidance??

Understand that we cannot manipulate God into giving us
guidance. But we can ask, seek, and knock.

Also, understand that God is very creative. Although He speaks
primarily through His Word, He can speak through a bumper
sticker, a child, an advertisement, or a sunset.

> *My sheep hear my voice,*
>   *and I know them,*
>   *and they follow me.*   John 10:27, ESV

---

[82] See my journal entry in Chapter 3 that includes the phrase, "My son, you
are forgiven."

Chapter 19: Testing Guidance

They came to us exuding strength and life - a young, handsome couple who wanted to help revitalize our aging congregation. Since we needed people like them, we welcomed them with open arms, and considered moving them quickly into leadership roles in worship and ministry. They, however, did not come alone. An older woman whom I will call Martha accompanied them; no, better, she managed them. Eventually we learned that she lived with them and directed their lives. We said to ourselves, "That's different;" but we needed vibrant, young couples, so we accepted the package.

Martha had a strong personality – nothing wrong with that; lots of people do. Following one of our worship services, we spent two hours together talking about the ministry and about our congregation. Some of her comments seemed fitting:

- I've listened to Charles Stanley for 30+ years. Why? Because he teaches the Bible.
- Healing comes only through the blood and power of Jesus.
- I probably will not come back after today. My instructions were to come here on Sunday and clear the land so that God can work here. I only go where Jesus sends me.
- I'm here to make sure that Thomas and his wife will be well cared for. I can see that they will.

Other comments bothered me:

- I will ask my spirit. When I ask my spirit, I'm asking the Holy Spirit.
- Thomas has great power. He's a golden dragon. (Thomas taught martial arts.)

- The "third eye."
- Their armies have been summoned to join my armies.
- I defeated 500 witches.

Following our conversation, Martha led us around the perimeter of our church campus and anointed it with oil, speaking words of praise and praying for protection.

I did not rest well that night.

A few days later, Martha asked me to take a rock from the canyon that was the color of the "third eye" and place it on my desk. She also gave me some special oil. "Rub this on your forehead," she said. "It will give you strength."

My uneasiness drove me to the Word, prayer, and trusted counselors.

The next morning, I smashed both the rock and the bottle of anointing oil in the name of our Triune God. Why? Because I felt that my heart was leaning toward dependence upon them and their supposed powers rather than on Jesus. Since I did not feel at peace about throwing the fragments into the trash container on our property, I drove to a nearby shopping center and threw them into an available dumpster. When I returned, I retraced our steps around our church campus and anointed the corners of our property in the Name of Jesus. I believe that Jesus has placed me in a position of spiritual authority here, not Martha or her students.

When I saw the young couple a week later, one of the godly matriarchs from our congregation happened to be with me. We all went into my office for conversation and prayer. While in prayer, this 75-year-old woman suddenly broke out into some of the strongest warfare prayer I've ever witnessed, mostly in tongues, telling the devil to go to hell. Later she told me that she rarely ever prays with such intensity.

Lessons Learned

In the spiritual realm, darkness and light are seldom black and white. Even our adversary is able to present himself as an angel of light (2 Corinthians 11:14). People who are good citizens and socially appropriate may be "plants" sent by the adversary to disrupt and destroy the church.

Four voices are able to press suggestions in our minds and hearts:

- God's (our Good Shepherd's)
- Our own
- Others
- The devil's

We need discernment to know whose voice we are hearing.

Four Tests

> *Beloved, do not believe every spirit, but test the spirits to see whether they are from God, for many false prophets have gone out into the world.*
> 1 John 4:1-6, ESV

Generally, I use a series of four questions which have been utilized for generations in various Christian circles as a starting point for determining what is of God and from God, and what is not.

1. Honor and exalt Jesus Christ

Does the teacher and teaching, the prophet and prophecy, the act and action honor and exalt Jesus Christ? John 12:32; 16:13-14

Guidance that is truly from God will honor and exalt Jesus Christ. We will be drawn toward Jesus more than we are toward a leader, a title (e.g., apostle, deacon, bishop), a charismatic personality, or a place (e.g., a sacred garden, an ancient burial ground).

2. Harmonize with Scripture

Is what is being said and done consistent with the intentions of God and the character of God as revealed in Scripture? 1 John 4:6; 1 Corinthians 14:37-38; 2 Timothy 3:14-17

The Holy Spirit will never lead us to do something that goes against Scripture.

The Pietists admired the Reformers' emphasis on the study of Scripture. The book that launched the Pietist movement, called *Pious Longings*, began with this plea: "There should be ... a more extensive use of the word of God among us." The author, Philip Spener, proceeded to argue that listening to good preaching isn't enough; believers need to be in the Word themselves. The Pietists called these small groups "conventicles," and they met on Sunday afternoons to discuss the passage that the pastor preached on that morning. The Pietists were people of the Word who filtered the voice of the Spirit through the grid of Scripture. They allowed for the possibility of direct "special revelations" apart from the Bible, but these revelations had to be tested by Scripture.[83]

We affirm with the Pietists that the Holy Spirit will only lead us to say and do things that harmonize with Scripture.

3. Confirmed by godly men and women

Do people who know their Bibles, are filled with the Holy Spirit, and are walking on the path of righteousness have an affirming witness? 1 Corinthians 14:29; 1 John 4:6

When I began to feel unsettled about Martha, I sent an email to a couple of our intercessors describing what was happening, and asking for feedback. Sharon responded by saying,

> I would keep my distance. Pray protection and the blood of the Lamb over yourself, your church, your family and your ministry. They cannot be a combination of the light and darkness. Their comments are occult in nature.

Another prayer partner wrote,

> Lots of red flags went up for me. Martha is from the wrong kingdom and is bringing evil into the church and using evil powers on the church. I can't say if she is a "plant," but I'm thinking so. "Plants" seek positions of

---

[83] Doug Banister, *The Word and Power Church* (Grand Rapids, MI: Zondervan, 1999), 46-47.

influence like mentoring, prayer groups, committee
leadership, and leadership with children; and work their
way up to the pastor. They may be faithful members
who contribute financially. They look good and it is
hard to expose them. They try to develop friendships,
so that others will defend them if necessary. Thus,
disunity arises. You are in big-time spiritual warfare as
Martha uses powers from darkness against you. Be alert
and very aggressive in the name of the Lord Jesus
Christ. Remember that words like "god, jesus, and
christ" may be used by persons with evil intent and are
not necessarily referring to the triune God whom we
worship.

The insights shared by these godly sisters helped me know how
to proceed.

4. Happens. Bears good fruit.

- Does what was predicted actually happen?
- Is there confirmation in objectively-verifiable events
  and facts? Deuteronomy 18:21-22; Isaiah 55:10-
  11; Jeremiah 32:6-9
- Does good fruit come from it?

Generally it takes time to witness the result of the guidance we
believe we are receiving. When the Holy Spirit is the source of
a word or action, it will come to pass.

Judy could not conceive, and more than anything she wanted a
natural-born child. One night she had a dream where she saw
herself in a delivery room giving birth to a son. Four months
later she got pregnant ... and had a daughter. "O well," she
thought, "I guess you miss some." She forgot the vision. Six
years later, she got pregnant again. In the delivery room, as the

doctor handed her baby boy to her, the whole vision came back, and she named him Peter.

Several years ago, Teri and I sensed that it was time to leave a ministry in which we were involved, and move on. At that time a good church in a desirable location invited me to come for an interview. As I prepared for the interview, the Lord nudged me to read John 15, and drew my attention to verse 16:

> *You did not choose me, but I chose you and appointed you to go and bear fruit – fruit that will last. Then the Father will give you whatever you ask in my name.*

On the day after learning that the search committee recommended us to the Elders for phase two of the interview process, during my regular Bible reading, the Lord highlighted Luke 5:11:

> *Then Jesus said to Simon, "Don't be afraid; from now on you will catch men." So they pulled their boats up on shore, left everything and followed him.*

Based on these verses I concluded that the Lord was guiding us to that church.

However, the search committee said, "No." To this day I do not know if they got it wrong, or if I did, or if we both did.

In June, 2001, while I was walking on the beach in Traverse City, Michigan, and praying, a phrase entered my mind and heart with a sense of urgency and forcefulness. It came to me as a combination of an invitation and a command.

> Ask of Me, and I will give you the nations as your inheritance.

"That's an odd phrase," I thought. "What does that have to do with anything?" Even though I did not know what it meant, in faith I began to consistently pray for the nations as an inheritance.

For more than four years I faithfully, and in faith, obeyed Jesus' invitation/command, asking Him for the nations as an inheritance. Four years later, as a result of a series of events, I received an invitation from the search committee of the Chinese Community Church in San Diego, California, for a face-to-face interview. Even though the Lord had given me a couple of indicators that He was weaving together a marvelous relationship with them, on the flight to San Diego I asked God for one more sign. As I prayed, I sensed in my spirit that if they were to include me in some way in their ground breaking event for their new building, that would be a clear indicator of God's will for me to serve as their pastor. Further, I sensed that I was to go beyond thinking about this possibility, to actually writing down this impression. I did.

At the ground breaking ceremony, everything proceeded as scheduled – prayers, singing, and speeches. I thought, "There's no way I will be included." Toward the end of the program, families and groups were getting their pictures taken holding shovels, and then heading out to a restaurant for lunch. At the last moment, Connie beckoned to me and said, "Phil, let's have our photographer take your picture holding a shovel, just in case it works out for you to come and serve as our pastor." Wow! For me that was a magnificent confirmation!

I returned to Traverse City. As the days wore on and we did not hear from San Diego, I began to doubt. I concluded that they must have settled on their other candidate. I felt despair, discouragement, and disappointment.

However, on Saturday, July 23, 2005, David, Connie, and John called to energetically invite me to return as their official candidate. "Do you accept?" they asked.

"Yes!!!"

I preached my first sermon at the Chinese Community Church as their new senior pastor on World Wide Communion Sunday, October 2, 2005.

> Ask of Me, and I will give you the nations as your inheritance.

If the answer is "Yes" to each to the four spiritual discernment questions, it is reasonably safe to conclude that the teacher and teaching, prophet and prophecy, leader and ministry, actor and action, are Biblically trustworthy.

Oswald Chambers counseled,

> There are times when you cannot understand why you cannot do what you want to do. When God brings the blank space, see that you do not fill it in, but wait. ... Never run before God's guidance.[84]

Tom Manesch observed wisely, "Generally, anointing follows obedience." Once we are sure that the guidance we received is from the Lord, the anointing to succeed will come as we step out in faith and obedience.

Elbert Hubbard advised, "Go as far as you can see, and when you get there, you'll see further."

---

[84] Oswald Chambers, *My Utmost for His Highest*, 1963. Reading for January 4.

Test the spirits. Not every deep-down good feeling is from God, and not every person who claims to be speaking truth and doing right actually is. Some are wolves in sheep's clothing. The Unity Church, for example, emphasizes goodwill and good deeds, but they miss the heart of the gospel. Learn to be discerning.

God convicts.

The adversary condemns.

God draws in love.

The enemy manipulates with fear.

Truth matters.

Chapter 20: Fruit First

She lined us up in front of her barn and demanded in an angry
voice with darting eyes, "Ok, who shot holes in my cupolas?"
For those who may not be familiar with the term, a cupola is a
small, dome-like fixture that sits on the roof of a barn or
similar structure and allows for ventilation. She had two, large,
metal cupolas attached high on the roof of her old, red barn – a
perfect roosting place for pigeons – and that's what my
brothers and I, along with a couple friends, were hunting. My
older brother said, "I did;" and even though I, too, had pulled
the trigger at least a dozen times, I remained silent.

Early patterns are hard to break. To this day, it is difficult for
me to stand like a man and accept full responsibility for my
choices and actions.

Someone wisely observed that our gifts can take us to heights
where our character cannot keep us. For some reason,
occasionally the Holy Spirit does for people in our day what
He did for Samson. Samson's personal life was a mess; yet,
God sovereignly chose to send the Holy Spirit upon him,
empowering him to accomplish great things. Eventually,
Samson had a great fall; and by God's grace, a great recovery.

We have all heard about Christian superstars who likewise
have had a great fall. For example, the San Diego Union
Tribune printed a story about Barry Minkow entitled, "Con

Man Gets Five Years in $3M Church Theft."[85] A con man with a deep knowledge of the Bible and dazzling oratory skills had become the pastor of a neighborhood church, and had used his skills to steal money from members of the congregation.

Sad, very sad.

The Biblical ideal is for both the fruit of the Spirit and the gifts of the Spirit to grow in our lives, with the fruit of the Spirit serving as the foundation upon which the gifts of the Spirit rest. Strong Christian character forged over time provides a firm foundation for power ministries.

An unknown author sagely observed, "God loves everyone, but definitely prefers 'spiritual fruits' over 'religious nuts!'"

---

[85] San Diego Union Tribune, Tuesday, April 29, 2014, front page.

David Watson said,

> All Word and no Spirit, we dry up;
> all Spirit and no Word, we blow up;
> both Word and Spirit, we grow up.[86]

Developing Christ-like Character

I believe that my mother's prayers propelled me to do it.
During my senior year in college, I set aside the dinner hour
most Sunday evenings for prayer and fasting. Or, maybe it was
my mother's prayers along with my tight budget. Sunday
evening dinners were not included in my college's meal plan.
In any event, on warm evenings I took my Bible, pen, and
notebook, and walked to a grassy knoll overlooking a quiet
pond. I invested the hour reading the Word and praying. On
cooler evenings, I found a quiet place in the library or dorm.
God used that discipline to build a foundation of integrity in
my life.

There are no shortcuts to spiritual maturity.

Eventually, I traveled to Pasadena to attend seminary. One day,
while walking across campus, I engaged in a little self-
examination. "Why," I wondered, "do so many aspects of the
Christian life feel like duty and not joy?" During the months
that followed, one of my main prayers for myself was simply
this:

> Lord Jesus, grow the fruit of "joy" in my life.

In time, He did.

---

[86] David Watson, *Christianity Today*, 10-22-01, page 40.

Several years later, I sat in my windowless office in the basement of our sanctuary in Traverse City, Michigan, wrapping up the day's work. For no explainable reason – other than God's transforming grace – my heart suddenly burst with joy! The Lord brought me back to that day in seminary when He led me to begin praying for joy, and I gave thanks – deep thanks.

Indeed, the Apostle Paul's words ring true:

> *We all, with unveiled face, beholding the glory of the Lord, <u>are being transformed</u> into the same image from one degree of glory to another. For this comes from the Lord who is the Spirit.* 2 Corinthians 3:18, ESV

Christianity is not merely an array of glorious ideas, nor is it the performance of rituals and sacraments. Rather, it includes deep, life-changing spiritual formation.

John Wooden's UCLA basketball teams won 10 NCAA championships in 12 years. One of his star players, Bill Walton, observed that Wooden's interest and goal was:

> To make you the best basketball player, yes, but first to make you the best person. He would never talk wins and losses but what we needed to succeed in life. Once you were a good human being, you had a chance to be a good player. He never deviated from that. He didn't teach basketball. He taught life.[87]

Character counts on the basketball court, in the family, in the community, and in life. Justification is the creation of a new person, and sanctification is the preservation, protection, and

[87] Gleaned from Hal Bock, Associated Press, "A Coach for All Seasons," The Spokane-Review Newspaper (12-4-00), C8.

development of that new person until the day of Christ's return. The same faith that results in justification is also the engine of sanctification.

> Spiritual formation is shaping the inner person in such a way that the words and deeds of Christ naturally flow from us. It is the inward transformation of the self that makes it easy and natural to do the things that Jesus said. ... Christian spiritual formation is the process [of becoming like Christ].[88]

Character formation occurs best in the context of safe communities that include men and women – like Coach Wooden, a devout Christian – who model the Person we are to become. However, even though good role models may not be available in the communities where we live, Jesus Christ – the perfect role model – always is. Study and imitate Him.

May the Grand Potter shape our inner beings to reflect Christ-like Christian character. The chief "shaper" is the Holy Spirit. Strong character forged over time supplies a firm foundation for power ministries.

We are all a work in progress. God isn't finished with us yet.

- Who are you?
- Who are you becoming?
- What are you doing to cooperate with Jesus to bring about even deeper levels of Christ-likeness in your life?

---

[88] Dallas Willard, speaking at a workshop entitled "Spiritual Formation for Real Life and Ministry in the 21st Century" at the National Pastors Convention, 2001. Quoted in an email from *Leadership Network*, Mar. 12, 2001.

Chapter 21: Deacon Philip: A Role Model of Spirit-Empowered Living

Now that I am in the sixth decade of my life, I realize that life unfolds in phases. When my wife and I were going through the kids-in-diapers phase, it seemed like it would last forever! But it didn't, thank God. Neither did the teaching-them-to-drive phase or the paying-college-tuition marathon. Phases come and phase go.

Most of the time, the passing of time (and a bundle of cash!) is all that is needed to transition from one phase to the next. For Spirit-filled believers, however, another dynamic is also at work; namely, the Holy Spirit. Philip serves as a good role model for Spirit-empowered living. According to the Book of Acts, his life unfolded in five phases.

Phase 1: Acts 6:1-7. Serving Tables in Jerusalem

As a result of the Church's growth, a conflict surfaced between the Hebrew Christians and the Hellenists regarding the care of their widows. Hebrew Christians were people who were born in Israel, spoke Aramaic and/or Hebrew, and preserved Jewish culture and customs. The Hellenists were Jews who were born in lands other than the Holy Land, and spoke Greek. When they became Christians, they tended to be more Greek than Hebrew in their attitudes and outlook.

To resolve the tension, the 12 apostles called the whole
community of disciples together for a press conference.

> *It is not right that we should give up preaching the*
> *word of God to serve tables. Therefore, brothers, pick*
> *out from among you seven men of good repute, full of*
> *the Spirit and of wisdom, whom we will appoint to this*
> *duty. But we will devote ourselves to prayer and to the*
> *ministry of the word.* Acts 6:2-4, ESV

The recommendation pleased everyone and they chose six
men, including Philip. The apostles commissioned the six to
their new roles by laying their hands on them and praying
(Acts 6:6), and the church continued to grow (Acts 6:7).

From these verses we learn that Philip not only passed the
character test – he had a good reputation – he also passed a
spiritual test – he was full of the Spirit, meaning in this context
that the Holy Spirit was at work within Philip to transform his
character.

During this phase of his life, Philip acted with coworkers,
under the authority of the apostles, to serve food to neglected
widows. What if Philip had not been faithful to this calling?
Would God have selected him for the ministry in Samaria??

Phase 2: Acts 8:4-13. Preaching to Crowds and
Performing Miracles in Samaria

Persecution forced many of the disciples to flee from Jerusalem
(Acts 8:1). Philip went to Samaria and proclaimed Christ to
them (Acts 8:5). He did not go there to perform signs and
wonders but to proclaim Christ. Nevertheless, signs and
wonders followed and reinforced his message. Crowds

gathered around him to listen and watch as unclean spirits fled with loud cries, and many who were paralyzed or lame were healed (Acts 8:4-13). The signs and wonders that accompanied the proclamation of the gospel convinced people that it was true. Scores of people believed and were baptized, and there was much joy in that city.

Phase 1 in Philip's life pertained to personal character building, and Phase 2 to evangelizing and power ministries. In due time, the Lord intervened to inaugurate the next phase.

Phase 3: Acts 8:26-39. Evangelizing One Person, an Ethiopian Eunuch, on a Desert Road

Things were going remarkably well in Samaria! So why did Philip leave that fruitful ministry and go to a desert road in the region of Gaza? Because he received guidance from God through an angel to go there (Acts 8:26). In obedience, he arose and went (Acts 8:27), a 40-50 mile journey. Philip did not hear from God again until after he had passed through Jerusalem and was well on his way down the dusty road toward Gaza. Perhaps many chariots were on the road at that time. We don't know; but we do know that the Spirit said to Philip:

Go over and join that chariot. Acts 8:29, ESV

Philip obeyed the Spirit's guidance, and that is the last record we have in Scripture of the Holy Spirit saying anything to him. From that point forward, logic and common sense kicked in and Philip shared Christ with the Ethiopian who, in turn, became a Christian. According to church history, that Ethiopian shared Christ with his boss, Candace. She, likewise, became a follower of Jesus and went on to evangelize in Ethiopia and the surrounding area.[89]

198

Phase 4: Acts 8:40. Traveling North to Caesarea, Preaching All the Way

> *But Philip found himself at Azotus, and as he passed through he preached the gospel to all the towns until he came to Caesarea.* Acts 8:40, ESV

Phase 5: Acts 21:8-9. Residing in Caesarea, Raising Godly Daughters

Scripture's last reference to Philip occurred 15-20 years after the conversion of the Ethiopian eunuch:

> *On the next day we departed and came to Caesarea, and we entered the house of Philip the evangelist, who was one of the seven, and stayed with him. He had four unmarried daughters, who prophesied.* Acts 21:8-9, ESV

With this brief statement, Scripture indicated that Philip allotted time to invest in his family. Why? Not because God gave him special guidance to do so. Rather, it appears that Philip determined that spending time with his family was the logical and responsible thing to do. When we read these verses we conclude that his four daughters not only knew Jesus; they were also in tune with the Holy Spirit to the degree that they exercised the spiritual gift of prophecy.

Good job, Dad!
Summation

---

[89] "Women in the Early Church," *Christian History*, Issue 17.

Most of the time Spirit-filled people live life by logic and common sense; that is, by a wisdom that is anchored in the written Word of God. We do not need special revelation to know that we are to spend quality time with our children or care for our aging parents. Sometimes, however, God intervenes in our lives in a manner similar to Philip's: He calls us to a specific task; He gives us a special assignment; e.g., "Go south to a desert road." Sometimes God's guidance draws one phase of our lives to a conclusion, and opens the door to a whole new quest. From God's perspective, every phase has eternal value and will have its own rewards.

- Today, if you hear His voice, do not harden your heart.

- But if you do not hear His voice, live by logic, common sense, and clear thinking that is anchored in Scripture.

That's how Spirit-filled people live.

Chapter 22: "But By My Spirit": How God Gets His Work Done

The first day that our mission team landed in Uganda, Africa, in June, 2014, we learned that the chairman of the Christian school we were resourcing had lost his father and that we were invited to the funeral. The next day we piled into the school's four-wheel-drive Toyota minivan and started toward our destination. A kilometer before arriving at the site of the funeral, we encountered a major obstacle. Our already bumpy, dirt road turned into a long stretch of water-filled ruts which were impassable. What should we do? Turn around and go back to the motel? No. We climbed out of the van and walked around puddles the remainder of the distance to a tent in an open field without electricity or running water where the pastor was preaching from an iPad!

Obstacles are a normal part of everyday life not only in Uganda but also in our lives, wherever we may live. However, when God has an objective that He wants accomplished, and when He determines to use us in the process, He will see to it that the obstacles that block our forward progress are removed or provide a way around them.

How does God get His work done in our world?

> *Not by might, nor by power, but by my Spirit, says the Lord of hosts.* Zechariah 4:6, ESV

One of God's strategies for removing obstacles and achieving His objectives is to pour fresh oil into chosen leaders thereby energizing and equipping them to mobilize others to do what He wants done. That's what God did in Zechariah's day, and that's what He is willing to do again … and again, in our day as well.

Although most of us intuitively know that we must depend on and cooperate with the Holy Spirit in order to get God's work done, we tend to settle for cheap substitutes.

Cheap Substitute #1: Instead of Depending on the Holy Spirit, we Rely on Ourselves

- Our energy
- Our skills
- Our education
- Our experience
- Our ingenuity and personality
- Our resources

We believe the lie that we can pay lip service to God, and still produce results that will honor Him. What often happens instead is that we slowly burn out. Tempers flare and tension fractures relationships.

Cheap Substitute #2: Instead of Depending on the Holy Spirit, We Rely on Other People and Other Things

During our brief time in Uganda, several people approached us with their needs: "If only I had a motorcycle," or "If only I had an acre of land and a few chickens, then my life would take a turn for the better." The not-so-subtle message behind their stories was a deep-seated belief that Americans are wealthy and that we have the resources to make the difficulties in their lives disappear.

As Americans, we are in a better position than they are but we are not their savior. Depending primarily on people instead of on God is a snare that will lead to disappointment and defeat.

Cheap Substitute #3: Instead of Depending on the Holy Spirit, We Rely on Modern Techniques

- High-tech equipment, sound systems, projectors, cameras, special lighting.
- Trendy wardrobes.
- High-powered staff members.
- Eye-catching websites.

None of these are wrong in and of themselves; but, when they become a substitute for depending on the Spirit of God, we are headed for trouble.   lot of wind and rain, but not much lasting fruit.

Francis Chan asks,

> Does your church feel more like what the prophets of Baal experienced before Elijah prayed? We can have a great time singing and dancing ourselves into frenzy. But at the end of it, fire doesn't come down from heaven. And people leave talking about the people who led rather than the power of God.[90]

---

[90] Francis Chan and Preston Sprinkle, *Erasing Hell* (David Cook, 2011), 184.

Our Limitations

I have been thinking about how limited I am, and how limited we are. The reality is this:

- We can plan a worship service, but we cannot give it wings.
- We can perform a wedding ceremony, but we cannot unite two hearts into one.
- We can exhort a sinner to repent, but we cannot convict him of his sin.
- We can address a negative attitude, but we cannot change it to a positive or produce deeper-level transformation.
- We can exhort an addict to change, but we cannot break his addiction.
- We can tell a person to "go to work," but we cannot magically create a job.
- We can share the gospel, but we cannot save anyone.
- We can plant a church, but we cannot cause it to thrive spiritually.
- We can teach about spiritual gifts, but we cannot impart or activate them.
- We can plan and lead a congregation, but we cannot build the Church.
- We can plant a seed, but we cannot make it grow.

Once again I quote Francis Chan:

> I bet you'd agree that a group of talented, charismatic leaders can draw a crowd. Find the right creative team, musicians, and speakers, and you can grow any church. It doesn't even have to be a Christian church. The fact

is that without making a conscious choice to depend on the Holy Spirit, we can do a lot.[91]

Yes, we can do a lot, but without the Holy Spirit we cannot:

- Touch a blind man's eyes and restore his sight.
- Soften a hard heart.
- Open a closed mind.
- Create within our community a hunger for God.
- Call down manna from heaven to feed hungry children.
- Forgive a sinner's sins or lift the weight of guilt from a brother's or sister's heart.

When it comes to doing real ministry, we quickly bump up against our limitations. We desperately need the oil of the Holy Spirit – fresh oil!

Several years ago, I participated in a conference where I was scheduled to teach on the "Nature and Experience of the Holy Spirit's Power." A few minutes before my talk, I searched through my briefcase but could not find my carefully-drafted lecture notes. I panicked. However, since I had a few power point slides, I decided to teach using them as prompts. God worked in amazing ways! I opened the topic; and, like popcorn, people began sharing stories that fit with the theme. Almost everything I had planned to say came through the mouths of others. There was "energy" in the room; we were together in the Spirit.

When I returned to my room that evening, I looked in my briefcase again. The notes were right there! Apparently God had blinded my eyes so that I, and we, would see His greater work. He enabled us as a group to experience that session's emphasis.

---

[91] Francis Chan and Preston Sprinkle, 181.

How does God get His work done?

> *Not by might,*
>   *nor by power,*
>   *but by my Spirit,*
>   *says the Lord of hosts.* Zechariah 4:6, ESV

Historical Context of Zechariah 4:6

Historically, during a span of about 1000 years, three temples were built in the nation of Israel.

- Solomon's temple was completed in 959 BC and remained standing for 373 years. In 586 BC, due to Judah's disobedience, God permitted the Babylonians to destroy it.

- In about 537 BC, approximately 70 years after Solomon's temple was destroyed, Zerubbabel began construction on a second temple, and dedicated it in 516 BC. It stood tall and strong for nearly 500 years.

- In 19 BC, Herod began to remodel Zerubbabel's temple. Jesus walked, taught, and performed miracles in Herod's temple. The Romans destroyed it in 70 AD.

Zechariah's proclamation, *Not by might, nor by power, but by my Spirit,* pertains to the construction phase of the second temple.

In 537 BC, God assigned to Zerubbabel, the Governor of Judah, the task of rebuilding the temple in Jerusalem. With great fanfare, they built the altar, and laid the foundation for the temple.

A year later (536 BC), the building project slowed, and by 520 BC, it stalled and stopped. At this low point, the Lord declared through the Prophet Zechariah to Zerubbabel:

> *Not by might, nor by power, but by my Spirit, says the Lord of hosts.*

What happened next? The building project re-started and four years later (516 BC), stood complete!

Anointed Leaders Made, and Make, the Difference

Why were they able to re-start and complete the Temple?

Because the Spirit of God anointed and empowered two men to give leadership to the building process:

- Zerubbabel the Governor
- Joshua the High Priest

God anointed them with His Spirit to function as leaders who would mobilize the people to complete the work that He wanted done.

The text described Zerubbabel and Joshua as the two "anointed ones" (Zechariah 4:14). According to the NetBible, the usual word for "anointed (one)," *mashiakh*, is not used here; rather, *vÿne-hayyitshar* which means literally, "sons of fresh oil."[92] Inserting these words into Zechariah 4:14 yields this

---

[92] https://net.bible.org/#!bible/Zechariah+4:8

translation: *"These are the two sons of fresh oil who stand by the Lord of the whole earth."*

In the Bible, "oil" is often used as a symbol of the Holy Spirit. As I began to comprehend this concept, my heart cried out,

"Lord, make me a son of fresh oil!"

"Lord, make us sons and daughters of fresh oil!"

Here's the point: The "fresh oil" of the Spirit re-energized Zerubbabel and Joshua as leaders; and, as re-energized leaders, they mobilized the people (the "lights," Zechariah 4:12), re-started the building process, and brought it to completion.

- In the process, the mountains (4:7), i.e., the obstacles, were leveled.
- In the end, the capstone (4:7), i.e., the final stone, was set in place.

Wow!

Relevance

One of God's primary strategies for getting His work done in our world is to pour fresh oil into and onto His sons and daughters thereby energizing and equipping them to advance His agenda.

Let's be more specific. Ask yourself, "Which of the projects that God has called me and/or us to do have stalled?"

Examples:
- To reach out to …
- To launch, to start …

208

- To design and build …
- To purchase ...
- To write …
- To lead …
- To support …

Perhaps we started strong but things have slowed down, even stopped.

If our projects are truly ordained by God, what might God do to re-start them? Based on Zechariah 4, He might pour the fresh oil of His Holy Spirit upon us just as He did upon Zerubbabel and Joshua, energizing us to complete our God-given assignments.

Ask Jesus for fresh oil. See what He does!

> *Not by might,*
> *nor by power,*
> *but by my Spirit,*
> *says the Lord of hosts.* Zechariah 4:6, ESV

For Further Reflection

Chapter 16: When Our Candle Becomes a Torch

1. Share a story about a time in your life and ministry when your candle became a torch.

2. As a result of reading this chapter, what longings or desires are being birthed by the Holy Spirit within you?

Chapter 17: Receiving Guidance

1. Share an example of God's guidance in your life.

2. Invite someone in the group to describe a situation where he or she personally needs God's guidance. As a small group, engage in a brief time of "listening prayer" for this person and their need. Following a period of silence in the Lord's presence, invite group members to share impressions, pictures, and/or words that the Holy Spirit has given to them.

3. What disciplines do you need to build into the routines of your week, and into the routines of your ministry's leadership team, in order to be in a better position to hear from Jesus?

Chapter 18: Testing Guidance

Apply the discernment criteria presented in this chapter to some event or experience in your life, family, or church; and draw a conclusion.

Chapter 19: Fruit First

1. Think about a few friends who knows you well. What character qualities would they affirm in your life, and what qualities might they suggest need to be developed further?

2. What routines and disciplines in your life are giving the Holy Spirit opportunities to transform you from the inside out?

Chapter 20: Deacon Philip: A Role Model of Spirit-Empowered Living

1. Describe the major phases in your life and talk about the events or circumstances that led to a transition from one phase to the next. Which phase(s) would you like to repeat? Why? Which do you wish you could delete? Why?

2. Currently, are you in transition? What might Jesus have for you next? How do you feel about that?

Chapter 21: "But By My Spirit:" How God Gets His Work Done

1. Think about an assignment that you have received from the Lord. What do you sense that Jesus is saying to you through Zechariah 4:6?

2. After a short time of discussion with your friend or group, spend an extended time in prayer. Include prayers of repentance and requests for fresh oil.

PART VI: ISSUES AND ANSWERS

Portions of the chapters that follow are more technical in nature. I encourage you to skim these pages and focus your reading on matters that interest you. Herein you will find many helpful insights into issues that historically have created confusion and division within Christian churches and denominations.

Chapter 23: Baptized with the Holy Spirit at Conversion?

Do regeneration and empowerment occur at the same time? When we are "born again" (converted), are we simultaneously baptized with the Holy Spirit and thereby empowered for greater witness and service?

Respected teacher and author John R.W. Stott argued that the only baptism with the Holy Spirit that any Christian will ever experience is the one that occurred when he or she was converted. Stott concluded that "the baptism of the Spirit is not a second and subsequent experience enjoyed by some

Christians but the initial experience enjoyed by all."[93] Stott described the baptism of the Spirit as something that is "received once for all at conversion," and the fullness of the Spirit as something "to be continuously and increasingly appropriated."[94]

Charles E. Hummel agrees with Stott, saying that the "Pentecostal (and, evangelical 'deeper life') doctrine of the baptism in the Spirit as a distinct second experience is not taught in the New Testament letters."[95] Hummel proceeds to declare that:

> For Paul, it [baptism with the Spirit] is a once and for all action of the Spirit at conversion incorporating the individual into the body of Christ.[96]

Hence, Hummel suggests, we need not seek or ask for a second work of grace. At the time of our conversion, the Holy Spirit equips us fully to advance the gospel.

Respected Bible teacher David Jeremiah adds his voice to Stott's and Hummel's:

> The baptism of the Holy Spirit is the imperceptible work of God by which the believing sinner is placed by the Holy Spirit into the body of Christ at the moment of salvation. ... The very process of the Spirit of God

---

[93] John Stott, *Baptism & Fullness: The Work of the Holy Spirit Today* (Downers Grove, IL: InterVarsity Press, Second Edition, 1975), 39. Stott's scholarly mind and pastor's heart have benefited me on many occasions. On this point, however, we differ.

[94] Ibid., 63.

[95] Charles Hummel, *Fire in the Fireplace* (Downers Grove, IL: InterVarsity Press, Second Edition 1979), 183. Generally, I hold Hummel in high esteem. On this point, however, we differ.

[96] Ibid., 184-185.

214

> placing you in the body of Christ is the baptism of the
> Holy Spirit. Nothing more, nothing less.[97]

If the authors quoted above are correct, then the implication
drawn by David Jeremiah is correct:

> What I want you to understand more than anything else
> is that the baptism of the Holy Spirit isn't the "second
> blessing." ... The filling of the Spirit is the second
> blessing and the twentieth blessing and the hundredth
> blessing!
>
> The baptism of the Holy Spirit isn't the second work of
> grace; it is rather what God has accomplished by
> placing you in the body of Christ.[98]

Are they correct? Are Christian men and women who hold
views contrary to theirs merely basing their beliefs on personal
experiences and not on Scripture?

A Key Verse: 1 Corinthians 12:13

A key verse that Stott, Hummel, and Jeremiah use to support
their position is 1 Corinthians 12:13:

> *For by[99] one Spirit we were all baptized into one body,
> whether Jews or Greeks, whether slaves or free, and we
> were all made to drink of one Spirit.* (NAS)

[97] David Jeremiah, *God in You* (Sisters, OR: Multnomah Publishers, 1998),
64-65.
[98] David Jeremiah, 74.
[99] The Greek word for "by" is *en*, which may be translated "in," "with," or
"by." See H.E. Dana and Julius R. Mantey, *A Manual Grammar of the
Greek New Testament* (The MacMillan Company, 1927, 1955), 105. I

Notice:

1. The repetition of "all."

Paul is not describing something that happened (and happens) to a privileged few; rather, an experience common to all believers.

2. The repetition of "one."

Knowing that many people in his audience in Corinth believed that many different spirits impacted their lives, Paul emphasizes that there is only one Holy Spirit and only one Body, not many spirits and many bodies. The Jews are not members of one body and the Greeks another. Slaves and free do not belong to a third and fourth body. Paul's big point is that all Christians are members of one Body, one Church, under one Head, Jesus Christ, and indwelt by one Spirit: the Holy Spirit.

> *... all were made to drink of one Spirit.*
> 1 Corinthians 12:13c, NAS

- When we drink water, it goes into us.
- When we are *"made to drink of one Spirit,"* He goes into us.

This verse (1 Corinthians 12:13) is teaching that two things happened simultaneously at the moment of our conversion:

   A. The Holy Spirit Himself plunges each of us into the one-body of Christ. *By one Spirit we were all baptized into one body ...* (12:13a, NAS)

---

believe that the NAS's choice of "by" fits best here.

B. The Holy Spirit Himself comes to live in each and every believer. *... and we were all made* [by Jesus] *to drink of one Spirit.* (12:13c, NAS). Cf. John 14:17; Romans 8:9; 1 Corinthians 6:19

Summation: The Big Picture

Three experiences are available:

1. The experience of being baptized (plunged) by the Holy Spirit into the Body of Christ, i.e., into the Church, into the family of God. 1 Corinthians 12:13a

2. The experience of being indwelt by the Holy Spirit. The Holy Spirit comes to live in us, 1 Corinthians 12:13c. It appears that Jesus is the one who sends the Holy Spirit to dwell in us.

3. The experience of being empowered by the Holy Spirit, i.e., being baptized with the Holy Spirit, for more effective witness and service. Acts 1:5, 1:8. Cf. Luke 24:49.

> *John baptized with water, but you will be <u>baptized with the Holy Spirit</u> not many days from now.* Acts 1:5, ESV.

> *You will receive power when the Holy Spirit has come <u>upon</u> you, and you will be my witnesses in Jerusalem and in all Judea and Samaria, and to the end of the earth.* Acts 1:8, ESV.

Empowerment may occur:

- at the moment of our conversion (e.g., Saul, Acts 9:17-19; and Cornelius, Acts 10:44-48)
- or at a later date (e.g., Jesus' disciples, John 20:22, and 50 days later, Acts 2:1-4).

Either pattern is possible in our day:

- Baptism with the Holy Spirit at the time of our conversion.
- Conversion first; then baptism with the Holy Spirit at a later date.

R.A. Torrey wrote:

> Again it is evident that the baptism with the Holy Spirit is an operation of the Holy Spirit, distinct from and additional to His regenerating work. A man may be regenerated by the Holy Spirit and still not be baptized with the Holy Spirit. In regeneration there is the impartation of life by the Spirit's power, and the one who receives it is saved; in baptism with the Holy Spirit, there is the impartation of power, and the one who receives it is fitted for service.[100]

---

[100] Long and McMurry, *Gateways,* 73-74, quoting R.A. Torrey.

218

Chapter 24: Critique of Cessationism

I grew up in a church culture where Cessationism was taught
and practiced. According to J.P. Moreland, Cessationism is the
belief that "the miraculous gifts of the Spirit, such as prophecy,
healing, miracles, and tongues (see 1 Corinthians 12:8-10;
13:8-10), ceased with the death of the apostles, and, thus, are
no longer available today."[101] Cessationists believe "that God
by His own will 'ceased' long ago to deal with His people in a
direct manner supernaturally. No more supernatural healings.
No visions. No direct revelation."[102] Cessationists love God
and they love Scripture, sound teaching, and holy living.
Nevertheless, they believe that, even though supernatural
events occurred frequently during a few phases in Old
Testament history, as well as in Jesus' day, they are rare in our
day – very, very rare. Why? Because of our lack of faith? Or
our failure to pray and fast? Or our low expectation level? Or
our failure to live holy lives? No. They believe that God
sovereignly chooses to work in our day through other means,
primarily through His written Word.

I no longer hold to the Cessationist's position.

---

[101] J.P. Moreland, *Kingdom Triangle* (Grand Rapids, MI: Zondervan, 2007),
175.
[102] R.T. Kendall, "When Believers Cease to Believe in the Supernatural" -
Charisma Magazine), May 29, 2014, 42.

I still remember the day when, following a careful study of 1 Corinthians 13:8-12, I came to the astonishing but settled conclusion that the interpretation of this key text, handed down to me by some of my respected teachers including John MacArthur, was wrong. "Is it ok," I asked myself with a mixture of apprehension and anticipation, "to disagree with a theological giant like John MacArthur?!?"[103]

Hinge Text #1: 1 Corinthians 13:8-12

The implications of one's interpretation of Paul's words in 1 Corinthians 13:8-12 are enormous. So important are these five verses that Wayne Grudem, in his *Systematic Theology* devoted 15 pages to discussing them (pages 1031-1046).

The central question we must answer is this: "Are all the gifts mentioned in the New Testament valid for use in the church today?"[104] This question arises from Paul's declaration in 1 Corinthians 13:8:

> *Love never ends.*
> *As for prophecies, they will pass away;*
> *as for tongues, they will cease;*
> *as for knowledge, it will pass away.* " (ESV)

In the context, Paul's objective, according to Wayne Grudem, is to "show that love is superior to gifts like prophecy because those gifts will pass away, but love will not pass away."[105]

A key question is this: "When will gifts such as prophecy, tongues, and words of knowledge pass away?"

---

[103] I continue to hold John MacArthur in high esteem. Regarding charismatic issues, however, we disagree.
[104] Wayne Grudem, *Systematic Theology* (Grand Rapids, MI, 1994), 1031.
[105] Wayne Grudem, 1032.

Answer:

>   *When the perfect comes, the partial will pass away.*
>   1 Corinthians 13:10, ESV

An important follow-up question is, "Who or what is the 'perfect' and when will he or it come?"

At this point paths diverge.

Cessationists' Answers

The "coming of the perfect" may be a reference to one of the following:

1. The completion of Scripture

Many people believe that the miraculous gifts of the Spirit ceased with the completion of the New Testament canon. They view the Book of Revelation, completed around 90 AD, as the final word from God, spoken or written. According to the ESV Study Bible:

>   The Cessationist view is that miraculous gifts such as prophecy, healing, tongues, interpretation, and miracles were given to authenticate the apostles and their writings in the early years of the church, but those gifts "ceased" once the entire New Testament was written and the apostles died (c. A.D. 100).[106]

2. When the gentiles are included in the church.

---

[106] *English Standard Version Study Bible*, 2211.

Gordon Fee wrote:

> Still others see it as referring to the maturing of the
> body, the church, which is sometimes also seen to have
> happened with the rise of the more regular clergy
> (Ephesians 4:11-13 is appealed to) or the coming of
> Jews and Gentiles into the one body.[107]

Critique and Response

Cessationists assume that every word a prophet speaks carries
the weight and authority of God and therefore must be added to
the Bible. Cessationists also remind us of the warning in
Revelation 22:18-19:

> *If anyone adds to them [the words of the prophecy of
> this book], God will add to him the plagues described
> in this book. "* (ESV)

Based on Revelation 22, they conclude that God finished
speaking at the end of the book of Revelation. Therefore, they
say, prophets and prophecy, tongues and interpretation are no
longer for today.

What Cessationists fail to recognize is that the New Testament
itself clearly distinguishes between the prophets of old (like
Jeremiah, Ezekiel, and Daniel), and people in our day who
have the spiritual gift of prophecy. Some (but not all) prophets
of old spoke the very words of God (2 Peter 1:20-21). Words
spoken by spiritually-gifted prophets in the New Testament
(and in our day) carry a lesser degree of authority. In fact,
according to 1 Corinthians 12:23, their words must be

---

[107] Gordon Fee, *The First Epistle to the Corinthians* (Grand Rapids, MI:
Eerdmans, Reprinted 1989), 645. Fee goes on to say that "This view has
nothing to commend to it."

"weighed" (evaluated; judged) by the Christian community in light of our standard, the Holy Bible. Hence, the words spoken by modern-day prophets are not on a par with the prophets of old and must not be added to the New Testament canon.

Who is the "Perfect"?

When the perfect comes, the partial will pass away.
1 Corinthians 13:10, ESV

The Charismatics' answer, along with the answer given by many Bible students (including myself) is this: The "perfect" in 1 Corinthians 13:10 is Jesus Christ, and the reference in this context is to His second coming. "The context (especially v.12) suggests strongly that Paul is referring here to the Second Coming of Christ as the final event in God's plan of redemption and revelation."[108] Spiritual gifts will cease when we see Jesus face to face (13:12) at His second coming.[109] To cite Barth's marvelous imagery: "Because the sun rises, all the lights will be extinguished."[110]

This understanding of 1 Corinthians 13:8-12 fits with Paul's statement in 1 Corinthians 1:7,

> *...you are not lacking in any gift, as you wait for the revealing of our Lord Jesus Christ.* (ESV)

---

[108] *Reformation Study Bible,* R.C. Sproul, General Editor, (Orlando, FL: Ligonier Ministries, 2005), 1662.
[109] Wayne Grudem, *Systematic Theology*, 1033. "The phrase 'see face to face' is several times used in the Old Testament to refer to seeing God personally – not fully or exhaustively, for no finite creature can ever do that, but personally and truly nonetheless."
[110] Gordon Fee, *Corinthians*, 646.

I agree with Wayne Grudem who expanded 1 Corinthians 13:10 to read, "But when Christ returns, prophecy and tongues (and other imperfect gifts) will pass away."[111] Between now and His advent on that glorious day, Paul expects every spiritual gift to continue – including tongues, interpretation, prophecy, healing, and miracles – for the building of the Body of Christ and advancement of the gospel. When Christ returns, all spiritual gifts will cease. Love will live on (1 Corinthians 13:8).

Hinge Text #2: Ephesians 2:19-20

> *So then you are no longer strangers and aliens, but you are fellow citizens with the saints and members of the household of God, built on the foundation of the apostles and prophets, Christ Jesus himself being the cornerstone.* Ephesians 2:19-20, ESV

Based on these words, many Cessationists assert that, by the end of the first century, the foundation of the Church was securely in place; hence, apostles and prophets ceased to function. Apostles and prophets completed their work of laying the foundation of the Church – a phase in the building process that needed to be done only once - and then they exited. Sam Storms summarized their view:

> Most Cessationists insist that, according to the analogy Paul employs, apostles and prophets belonged to the period of the foundation of the church and not its superstructure. That is to say, these two groups and their respective gifts were designed by God to operate only during the early years of the church's existence in order to lay the once-for-all foundation.[112]

---

[111] Gordon Fee, *Corinthians*, 1035.

Response

I agree with the Charismatic who respond by saying:

1. God used a select group of apostles and prophets to pen
Scripture. Thank God for His living and abiding Word! The
cannon of Scripture is closed: no new contributions are being
accepted.

2. The Church is founded primarily on Jesus Christ and
secondarily on the Apostles and Prophets.

3. However, not every word that an apostle (small "a") or
prophet (small "p") speaks in our day must be included in
Scripture. For the sake of illustration, let's suppose that the
total number of apostles and prophets in the first century was
50. How many of them contributed to the New Testament
canon? Maybe five or six.

The Prophet Joel envisioned a day when many people would
prophesy, dream dreams, and see visions (Joel 2:28-29; Acts
2:17-18). In Ephesus (Acts 19:6-7), twelve men spoke in
tongues and prophesied, but none of their words are recorded
in Scripture. Philip the evangelist had four unmarried daughters
who prophesied (Acts 21:8-9), but none of their words are
recorded in Scripture.

Charismatics contend that, even though God speaks primarily
through His written Word, He also reveals things in our day to
His people through legitimate prophets and prophecies. As we

---

[112] Sam Storms, *Strange Fire and the Cessationist Attack* (Charisma
Magazine, 2014), 49-50.

noted above, what a prophet says needs to be evaluated in light of Scripture before it is received as a word from the Lord.[113]

Summary of Implications

- If we side with the Cessationist's interpretation and conclude that manifestational gifts such as prophecy, tongues, miracles, and healing are no longer for today, then we must shut down the expression of these gifts in our lives and in our churches in America and around the world.

- If we side with the Charismatic's interpretation and affirm that legitimate expressions of all the spiritual gifts included in Scripture are available to Christians today, then we will anticipate and welcome them in our lives and in our churches.

Personally, I side with the Charismatics on this issue.

But what about abuses?

Yes, there have been, are, and will be abuses of tongues, prophecy, and healing; but, the abuse of a spiritual gift does not invalidate the gift itself. Legitimate, Biblical expressions of all the spiritual gifts in Scripture – and possibly more, such as a special capacity to lead worship – are available to Christians today.

Regarding the experiential dimension of the Holy Spirit's work, in 1984, John Piper observed that many Christians today believe in the Holy Spirit, but they do not experience Him.

---

[113] In order to discern the wheat and discard the chaff, the spiritual gift of prophecy deserves much more study than we are giving it in this chapter.

They accept by faith that He is working, but they do not see or sense His presence. Piper proceeded to say,

> But that is far from what we see in the New Testament. The Pentecostals are right to stress the experience of being baptized in the Spirit. ...

> I sometimes fear that we have so redefined conversion in terms of human decisions and have so removed any necessity of the experience of God's Spirit, that many people think they are saved when in fact they only have Christian ideas in their head, not spiritual power in their heart. ...

> So you see, the real issue the Charismatics raise for us is not the issue of tongues. In itself that is relatively unimportant. The really valuable contribution of the Charismatic renewal is their relentless emphasis on the truth that receiving the gift of the Holy Spirit is a real, life-changing experience.

> Christianity is not merely an array of glorious ideas. It is not merely the performance of rituals and sacraments.

> It is the life-changing experience of the Holy Spirit through faith in Jesus Christ the Lord of the universe.[114]

Charity Needed

---

[114] John Piper, http://www.adrian.warnock.info/2005/09/piper-on-baptism-with-holy-spirit.htm

Within the bigger circle of Christians and Christianity, many streams flow, each with its particular emphasis and practice. Why? Because the Word of God is both clear and complex. Generally, true Christians agree on clear issues – core issues – but often differ on the meaning of complex Biblical texts, some of which are secondary. If we all agreed on everything we would not have Baptists, Methodists, Presbyterians, Calvinists, Armenians, and Pentecostals. However, each of these groups has their "spin" on the correct way to interpret difficult texts. I expect that, from God's point of view, each group's doctrine includes a mixture of truth and error. No group can legitimately say, "We are right, and everyone who disagrees with us is wrong."

People who are serving in leadership roles within a particular group (e.g., Baptists) need to affirm and abide by the theological "spin" and practice of the Baptists, or switch to a stream that is more in harmony with their personal convictions. The same is true for Pentecostals.

Our task is not to demonize other Christian people or groups simply because they do not agree with us. As long as they affirm core Christian doctrines – such as the divinity of Jesus Christ, the authority of Scripture, sin, and salvation – we applaud their efforts to advance the gospel even if we disagree on secondary issues such as speaking in tongues, prophecy, and healing. Further, we must remain teachable. We must be willing to learn from thoughtful interactions with fish that swim in other Christian streams.

Relevance

After I came to the conclusion that I sided with the Charismatic interpretation of 1 Corinthians 13:8-12 and Ephesians 2:19-20, what happened? Jesus began to slowly but surely work in my life in some wonderful and refreshing ways. Two examples:

1. Years ago, I felt very uncomfortable in small group prayer gatherings when someone quietly expressed a prayer in tongues. Likewise, a prophetic word spoken in the context of a larger group left me feeling unsettled. I now hear and receive tongues and prophecy not only as normal but also as reassurance that Jesus truly is among us. He is helping us pray (Romans 8:26-28) and building us up (1 Corinthians 14:3).

2. During our worship service a few weeks ago, we as a congregation lifted our voices in praise. Suddenly the Holy Spirit surged within me and I began to quietly speak in tongues as the congregation continued singing. No one else knew, but I rejoiced as the Spirit flowed because I knew that Jesus was equipping me to teach.

> *The one who speaks in a tongue builds up himself.*
> 1 Corinthians 14:4, ESV

On numerous occasions during recent years I have had similar experiences, for which I thank God.

Come, Holy Spirit, come!

Chapter 25: The Dual Meaning of "Filled"

The English Standard Version's translation of Luke's account of Pentecost uses the word "filled" twice. Notice, however, that the Greek words behind these English words are different.

> When the day of Pentecost arrived, they were all together in one place. 2 And suddenly there came from heaven a sound like a mighty rushing wind, and it _filled_ (play-ro-o) the entire house where they were sitting. 3 And divided tongues as of fire appeared to them and rested on each one of them. 4 And they were all _filled_ (pim-play-me) with the Holy Spirit and began to speak in other tongues as the Spirit gave them utterance. Acts 2:1-4, ESV

An understanding of the difference in meaning between the Greek words that are translated "filled" untangles a great deal of confusion pertaining to the empowering dimension of the Holy Spirit's work. A side-by-side comparison looks like this:

230

play-ro-o and *play-race*	*pim-play-me*
Describes a long-term state-of-being. Example: A tree is filled with sap. Pertains to: • The Holy Spirit "within" for inner transformation. • Long-term filling for sanctification. Is *not* followed by dramatic action.	Describes a temporary, episodic filling. Pertains to a short-term filling with the Holy Spirit that results in dynamic action. The Holy Spirit works powerfully through us, energizing our words and/or works to advance Jesus' agenda for a person or situation. Then He "lifts."

In Acts 1:4, for example, the Holy Spirit's filling led to dynamic action:

> They were all _filled_ (pim-play-me) with the Holy Spirit and _began to speak in other tongues_ as the Spirit gave them utterance. Acts 2:1-4, ESV

Let's take a closer look at several New Testament texts.

Full, Filled: *Play-ro-o*[115] and *Play-race*[116]

---

[115] **Play-ro-o**. [To simplify our study I am writing these Greek words phonetically.]
• Bower, Arndt, and Gingrich, 676: 1. Make full, fill (full). A. of things. B. of persons (fill with powers, qualities, etc.).
• Strong's #4137, derived from #4134. Occurs 90 times in the New

Generally, in the texts that follow, "full" and "filled" do not lead to, or result in, dynamic action. Rather, the texts describe a state of being.

- *When it was _full_ (play-ro-o) [of fish], men drew it ashore and sat down and sorted the good into containers but threw away the bad.*
  Matthew 13:48, ESV

- *The house was _filled_ [play-ro-o] with the fragrance of the perfume.* John 12:3, ESV

- *You have made known to me the paths of life; you will make me _full_ [play-ro-o] of gladness with your presence.* Acts 2:28, ESV

- *"We strictly charged you not to teach in this name, yet here you have _filled_ [play-ro-o] Jerusalem with your teaching."* Acts 5:28, ESV

- *The disciples were filled [play-ro-o] with joy and with the Holy Spirit.* Acts 13:52, ESV

Testament. Meaning: 1. to make full, to fill up, i.e. to fill to the full. 1a) to cause to abound, to furnish or supply liberally. 1a1) I abound, I am liberally supplied. 2) to render full, i.e. to complete. 2a) to fill to the top: so that nothing shall be wanting to full measure, fill to the brim. https://net.bible.org

[116] *Play-race*
- Bower, Arndt, and Gingrich, 675. filled, full.
- Strong's #4134, derived from #4130. Occurs 17 times. Meaning: 1) full, i.e. filled up (as opposed to empty). 1a) of hollow vessels. 1b) of a surface, covered in every part. 1c) of the soul, thoroughly permeated with. 2) full, i.e. complete. 2a) lacking nothing, perfect. https://net.bible.org

In the above instances the words "full" and "filled" describe a longer-term state of being that is not followed by dynamic action. Rather, we find a description of what is. The net was full of fish. The perfume's fragrance filled the house. The disciples were filled with joy.

Likewise, the following references to Jesus and the disciples describe a state of being "full," but the fullness does not lead to, or result in, dynamic action. In general, these references are to the Holy Spirit's inward work.

- *And Jesus, full [play-race] of the Holy Spirit, returned from the Jordan and was led by the Spirit in the wilderness.* Luke 4:1, ESV

- *Suddenly there came from heaven a sound like a mighty rushing wind, and it filled (play-ro-o) the entire house where they were sitting.* Acts 2:2, ESV

- *For in him the whole fullness [play-ro-mah] of deity dwells bodily, 10 and you have been filled [play-ro-o] in him, who is the head of all rule and authority.* Colossians 2:9-10, ESV

- *Therefore, brothers, pick out from among you seven men of good repute, full [play-race] of the Spirit and of wisdom.* Acts 6:3, ESV

- *And they chose Stephen, a man full [play-race] of faith and of the Holy Spirit.* Acts 6:5, ESV

- *But he, full [play-race] of the Holy Spirit, gazed into heaven and saw the glory of God, and Jesus standing at the right hand of God.* Acts 7:55, ESV

- *... for he [Barnabas] was a good man, <u>full</u> [play-race] of the Holy Spirit and of faith.* Acts 11:24, ESV

Fill, Full: *Pim-play-me*[117]

Pim-play-me is also translated with our English word "fill," or "full." In contrast to the above texts, *pim-play-me* <u>usually leads to quick and dramatic action.</u>

- *Elizabeth was <u>filled</u> [pim-play-me] with the Holy Spirit, 42 and she <u>exclaimed</u> with a loud cry, "Blessed are you among women, and blessed is the fruit of your womb!"* Luke 1:41-42, ESV

- *His father Zechariah was <u>filled</u> [pim-play-me] with the Holy Spirit and <u>prophesied.</u>* Luke 1:67, ESV

Summation

A review of the words in Scripture for "filled" leads us to once again describe two basic operations of the Holy Spirit:

1. The transforming work of the Holy Spirit: long-term filling for character development.

The Holy Spirit lives within each and every Christian developing Christ-like character qualities; namely, the fruit of the Spirit. Compelled by Christ's love, we do much good and advance the gospel for the glory of God.

---

[117] Bower, Arndt, Gingrich, 66.: fill, fulfill. Note: Strong and Bauer (BAG) use two different spellings for the same word: Strong, play-tho; and BAG, pim-play-me. Strong's #4130, states that play-tho occurs 24 times in the New Testament and means 1) to fill. 2) to be fulfilled, to be filled. See BAG, 678, which indicates that pim-play-me may also be spelled play-sas or play-stheis.

2. The empowering work of the Holy Spirit: short-term filling for *kairos* moments.

The Holy Spirit comes "upon" us from above. He moves from outside of us to inside, and fills us full. He clothes Himself with us thereby equipping us to advance God's agenda for that situation at that moment in time. He activates and releases the spiritual authority, power, and gifts that we need – specifically, the manifestational gifts of the Spirit as recorded in 1 Corinthians 12:7-11 – to successfully fulfill our mission. Then, He lifts.

Let this be our prayer:

> Father in heaven, with greater frequency and greater measure, send Your Holy Spirit upon me, equipping and empowering me for ministry in general and for every specific ministry to which You call me, enabling me to advance Your agenda for Your glory.

Filled and Filled Again

In Acts 2:4, *pim-play-me* led quickly to dynamic action – they spoke in tongues. Following that, Peter preached and 3,000 people were converted (Acts 2:41).

A few chapters later in the Book of Acts, the same people who had been filled (*pim-play-me*) with the Spirit on the Day of Pentecost were filled again … and again, demonstrating the episodic nature of empowerment.

- *Then Peter, <u>filled</u> (pim-play-me) with the Holy Spirit, <u>said</u> to them, "Rulers of the people and elders …."*
  Acts 4:8, ESV

- *When they had prayed, the place in which they were gathered together was shaken, and they were all filled (pim-play-me) with the Holy Spirit and continued to speak the word of God with boldness.* Acts 4:31, ESV

I believe that Jesus intends for a similar pattern to occur in our lives. Our initial baptism with the Holy Spirit is not a once-in-a-life-time solution; rather, it is our initiation into the empowering dimension of the Holy Spirit's work. It establishes a capacity for the Holy Spirit to come "upon" us again and again to advance God's agendas in new situations.

Saul/Paul's life provides another example of the episodic nature of empowerment.

- Saul's baptism with the Holy Spirit

  > *Brother Saul, the Lord Jesus who appeared to you on the road by which you came has sent me so that you may regain your sight and be filled (pim-play-me) with the Holy Spirit. 18 And immediately something like scales fell from his eyes, and he regained his sight.* Acts 9:17-18, ESV

- In a subsequent ministry context, Jesus again filled Saul/Paul with the Holy Spirit, empowering him to deal with a difficult person.

  > *But Saul, who was also called Paul, filled (pim-play-me) with the Holy Spirit, looked intently at him and said, "You son of the devil ...."* Acts 13:9-10, ESV

The point is this: once we are empowered we do not live in an empowered state.[118] Empowerment is episodic in our day just

236

as it was in the Old Testament and the New. The Holy Spirit falls upon us on an "as needed" basis. When we engage in ministry in response to the Holy Spirit's guidance, Jesus sends His Spirit upon us to empower us to do the work He wants done. When Jesus' work through us for that occasion has been completed, the Spirit "lifts."

I do not understand all the dynamics of empowerment; it includes mystery. Sometimes God takes the initiative to empower us without our asking. On other occasions, He waits for us to cry out to Him for help. Obviously, we are not in control of the Holy Spirit. He is sovereign and He will do what He will do, when He wants to do it.

In May, 2003, I noted the following in my journal:

> During one of our initial times of worship on Sunday evening, I "saw" the heavens open for a moment and something like a mingling of light and raindrops being poured into me as if from a heavenly watering can. It happened so quickly and quietly that I almost missed it. Yet I know that I know that in the spiritual realm, it happened. "What is God doing?" I wondered. In retrospect I believe that He was letting me know that He was pouring out a fresh measure of the Holy Spirit upon me, equipping me to serve Him well during the remainder of the conference.

In November, 2009, I had a similar experience. During the Saturday evening worship time (preceding our ministry time), I felt a need for prayer. As the singing continued, the Lord directed my attention to Judy. I sat down beside her and said, "I'm feeling a need for prayer. Can you pray for me?" She immediately lifted her right hand high above my head and

---

[118] Exception: Jesus

lowered it toward me. As she did, I "saw" (and felt) a sensation like glitter raining down upon me. Judy startled and said, "Wow! Did you feel that?!?" In retrospect, I believe that Jesus was equipping me to participate in a deliverance ministry that would occur later that evening.

Both '"In" and "Upon"

Brad Long summarized the themes in this chapter when he observed,

> Being filled with the Holy Spirit then really has two different meanings, depending on the context. The Spirit is to be within us transforming our character to be more and more Christ-like. At the same time, we may have the Holy Spirit upon us for power, manifesting the gifts and doing the works that Christ did.[119]

Wise people endeavor to grow in both ways so that Jesus may be glorified.

---

[119] Long and McMurry, *Gateways*, 234.

Ephesians 5:18: "Be Filled with the Spirit"

> *Do not get drunk with wine, for that is debauchery,
> but be filled (play-ro-o) with the Spirit.*
> Ephesians 5:18, ESV

Honestly, I am continuing to wrestle with Paul's original intent when he penned the phrase, *be filled with the Spirit.* Each of the two different meanings of this verse, as presented in what follows, seem plausible. Paul's true intent may be a combination of both.

1. *Be filled (play-ro-o) with the Spirit:* Long-term filling for character transformation

Let's assume that Paul, under the inspiration of the Holy Spirit, chose his words carefully and that he used them consistently. If this is the case, we must define the word "filled" in Ephesians 5:18 (*play-ro-o*) in a way that harmonizes with other contexts that use the same word. In other contexts, as we noted above, *play-ro-o* generally described long-term filling for inner transformation, and these fillings were not accompanied by dramatic displays of power. This meaning fits with the long-term, relational, body-building outcomes that Paul listed in Ephesians 5:19ff.:

- songs, hymns, spiritual songs
- a thankful heart
- mutual submission
- orderly relationships

2. *Be filled (play-ro-o) with the Spirit:* Short-term filling for power ministry

"Why," I wondered, "didn't the Apostle Paul or the Apostle Peter use the phrase "baptism with the Holy Spirit" in any of their writings? From Paul's perspective, was the Luke-Acts experience of Spirit-baptism confined to the birth of the early Church? Once the Church was up and running, was baptism with the Holy Spirit no longer necessary for the spread of the gospel? And hence, is baptism with the Holy Spirit no longer essential in our day?"

Since these questions troubled me, I decided to re-read the 13 epistles and letters that the Apostle Paul wrote, and highlight references to power ministry. Here is a sample of what I found:

- *I will not venture to speak of anything except what Christ has accomplished through me to bring the Gentiles to obedience—by word and deed, by the power of signs and wonders, by the power of the Spirit of God—so that from Jerusalem and all the way around to Illyricum I have fulfilled the ministry of the gospel of Christ.* Romans 15:18-19, ESV

- *I was with you in weakness and in fear and much trembling, and my speech and my message were not in plausible words of wisdom, but in demonstration of the Spirit and of power, so that your faith might not rest in the wisdom of men but in the power of God.* 1 Corinthians 2:3-5, ESV

- *The signs of a true apostle were performed among you with utmost patience, with signs and wonders and mighty works.* 2 Corinthians 12:12, ESV

- *For we know, brothers loved by God, that he has chosen you, 5 because our gospel came to you <u>not only in word</u>, <u>but also in power</u> and in the Holy Spirit and with full conviction. You know what kind of men we proved to be among you for your sake.* 1 Thessalonians 1:4-5, ESV

Clearly the Apostle Paul believed and practiced the power dimension of the Holy Spirit's work. However, he did not use the phrase "baptism with the Holy Spirit," nor did he exhort new converts to be baptized with the Holy Spirit.

After reading His letters, it occurred to me that, while Paul practiced power ministries, he emphasized other themes in his writings such as justification, sanctification, Christian living, healthy relationships, spiritual warfare, and missions. Examples:

- *Therefore, since we have been <u>justified by faith</u>, we have peace with God through our Lord Jesus Christ.* Romans 5:1, ESV

- *Let each of you look not only to his own interests, but also <u>to the interests of others</u>.* Philippians 2:4, ESV

- *Therefore, my beloved, as you have always obeyed, so now, not only as in my presence but much more in my absence, <u>work out your own salvation</u> with fear and trembling, for it is God who works in you, both to will and to work for his good pleasure.* Philippians 2:12-13, ESV

- *But as for you, O man of God, flee these things. <u>Pursue righteousness, godliness, faith, love, steadfastness, gentleness</u>.* 1 Timothy 6:11, ESV

- *Show yourself in all respects to be a <u>model of good works</u>, and in your teaching show integrity, dignity, and sound speech that cannot be condemned, so that an opponent may be put to shame, having nothing evil to say about us.* Titus 2:7-8, ESV

My core question remained unanswered: "Was baptism with the Holy Spirit only for the people who were present on the Day of Pentecost? Did Paul expect Christians in his day, and in our day, to fulfill our mandate in Act 1:8 without the Holy Spirit's empowerment?"

A turning point came during a lunch conversation with a retired professor of New Testament from Asbury Theological Seminary. By chance – or better, by God's design – when I walked into the room, the chair next to him was open and I was ushered to it. I had no idea who he was, but after learning of his credentials, we engaged in conversation.

"As I understand it," I said, "Asbury Seminary places a strong emphasis on the Holy Spirit."

"That is correct," he replied.

"May I ask you a question?"

"Sure, go ahead."

"I have been thinking about the baptism with the Holy Spirit. Clearly, John the Baptist used the phrase, and so did Jesus, but I cannot find it in Paul's writings."

"That is not true," he replied, "It is in Paul's writings too. Look at Ephesians 5:18: *Do not get drunk with wine, for that is debauchery, but be filled with the Spirit.*

I thanked him and continued to ponder the issue. Later that afternoon I experienced an "ah-ha" moment.

As we noted earlier, on the Day of Pentecost the Holy Spirit moved:

1. From above the 120 prayer warriors who were assembled in the upper room (*And suddenly there came from heaven a sound like a mighty rushing wind,* Acts 2:2, ESV)

2. To upon them (*and divided tongues as of fire appeared to them and rested on each one of them.* Acts 2:3, ESV)

3. To within them *("And they were all filled with the Holy Spirit,"* Acts 2:4, ESV).

Even though Luke did not summarize and say, "And thus they were all baptized with the Holy Spirit," it is clear that the three-step process described in Acts 2:1-4 was the outworking of Jesus' promise ten days earlier:

> *... for John baptized with water, but you will be baptized with the Holy Spirit not many days from now.* Acts 1:5, ESV

Fast-forward to the phrase Paul used: *Do not get drunk with wine, for that is debauchery, but be filled with the Spirit,* Ephesians 5:18, ESV. When referring to empowerment, Luke used one Greek word for "filled" (Acts 2:4, *pim-play-me*); and in Ephesians 5:18, Paul used another (*play-ro-o*). Could it be that the net result in this context was, and is, the same?? Could it be that those who are filled with the Spirit are controlled by the Spirit, and that sometimes the Spirit who controls them chooses to work powerfully through them to advance the Father's agenda??

A side-by-side comparison suggests that the answer is "Yes."

Acts 2:1-4 Jesus' Promise Fulfilled	Ephesians 5:18 Paul's Exhortation
From heaven	
Rested on	
Filled with the Holy Spirit.	Be filled with the Holy Spirit.

It appears that, in Ephesians 5:18, the Apostle Paul truncated the Pentecost process and focused on the end result of the Spirit-baptism, namely, the control that the Holy Spirit exercises in, and over, the people whom He fills.

Continuously Filled? Or, Repeatedly Filled?

One more question puzzled me about Paul's exhortation in Ephesians 5:18. "Are we to be continuously filled with the Holy Spirit, even when we are watching a football game, walking the dog, or driving home after a long day at work? Or, are we to ask Jesus for a fresh infilling for every new ministry opportunity that the Lord puts in our path?"

In Ephesians 5:18, the verb "be filled" is a present passive imperative.

- The present tense calls for a habitual and continuing action.[120] Carson translated it "be being filled with the Spirit."[121]

---

[120] Reinecker and Rogers, 538.

244

- An imperative is a command.

- The passive voice indicates that someone from outside of us is acting on us; in this case, that someone is God.[122] In this context, Paul may be using the permissive passive, "allow yourselves to be filled with the Spirit"[123] As believers, we do not fill ourselves with the Holy Spirit but we allow ourselves to be filled with Him. The Holy Spirit will not override free will. As we saw in earlier chapters, the Spirit may be resisted (Acts 7:51), quenched (1Thessalonians 5:19), and grieved (Ephesians 4:30). Here, Paul exhorts us to turn from these negative responses, and invite the Holy Spirit to fill us and control us completely.

Michael Green believed that the Apostle Paul intends for us to be continuously filled with the Holy Spirit.

Thus, while baptism in the Spirit is the initial experience of Christ brought about by the Spirit in response to repentance, faith, and baptism, the fullness of the Holy Spirit is intended to be the continual state of the Christian.[124]

In contrast, the NIV Study Bible interprets Paul to mean "be repeatedly filled with the Holy Spirit."

---

121 D.A. Carson, Showing the Spirit: *A Theological Exposition of 1 Corinthians 12-14* (Grand Rapids, MI: Baker Book House, Fourth Printing, July 1992), 159.
122 Colin Brown, Ed., *The New International Dictionary of New Testament Theology* (Fourth Printing, Oct. 1979), 738.
123 Reinecker and Rogers, 538.
124 Michael Green, *I Believe in the Holy Spirit* (Grand Rapids, MI: Eerdmans, 1977), 185-186.

> The Greek present tense is used to indicate that the filling of the Spirit is not a once-for-all experience. Repeatedly, as the occasion requires, the Spirit empowers for worship, service, and testimony.[125]

In other words, the Spirit's work is episodic. In each new ministry setting, we ask for a fresh anointing (filling) with the Holy Spirit. This fits with Paul's earlier reference to wine. When we are filled with wine, we are controlled by the wine. Very few people, however, are continuously drunk; rather, they get drunk, then sober; drunk, then sober; and the cycle continues. Hence, Paul is exhorting us to "be repeatedly filled with (empowered by; under the control of; clothed with) the Holy Spirit."

Summation of Ephesians 5:18

- Being continuously filled with the Holy Spirit leads toward inner transformation. Invite the Holy Spirit, who always dwells in you, to fill you, and transform you to become more and more like Jesus Christ.

- Being repeatedly filled with the Holy Spirit leads toward repeated experiences of empowerment. In each new ministry situation, yield yourself totally to the Holy Spirit, allowing Him to fill you once again and work powerfully through you to advance His agenda.

Analogies for being filled with the Spirit

The following analogies help me understand what it means to be filled with the Holy Spirit.

---

[125] *NIV Study Bible*, 1798.

1. Big house, many rooms

When we become Christians we open the door of the house of our lives and invite Jesus in. He comes into one of the rooms and dwells there, but the doors to the other rooms remain closed. Jesus and the Holy Spirit are present in our lives but they not present in fullness. When we humbly open the other doors and invite Him into every room, we experience His fullness.

2. Gas log fireplace

In a gas log fireplace the pilot light is always on but it is not generating much heat. When we turn up the thermostat, we experience the warmth of the full flame.

3. Alka-Seltzer

If we leave the wrapper on an Alka-Seltzer tablet and drop it in a glass of water, not much happens. However, when we remove the wrapper and drop the tablet in, the water fizzes and bubbles.

Regarding the meaning of "filled," Tony Evans presented a helpful analogy:

> The moment you pull away from the filling station, dissipation occurs. As you drive, you use up the gasoline. Over time you will burn gas. The length of time from full to empty depends on how far you travel, how fast you travel, and the amount of air-conditioning or heat used. The fuel indicator slowly goes from full to

empty because driving the car uses the energy the fuel provides. Eventually the car will need to be filled up again with gasoline. The filling of a car is an ongoing responsibility.

In the same way, as we live life we get drained spiritually. We go to church, have our devotions, and spend time in fellowship with other Christian believers so that we can fill our tanks. But as we live our lives, we run empty as we expend our spiritual energy doing the work God has for us. In order to continue to do the work, we have to continue to get refilled.[126]

D L Moody was once asked why he repeatedly urged Christians to be filled with the Holy Spirit. He replied, "I need a continual infilling because I leak!" He pointed to a water tank which had sprung a leak. "I'm like that!" he said.

What can we say in summary?

Be filled with the Holy Spirit!

As we enter into each new day and/or new ministry situation, let this be our prayer:

Lord Jesus, I lay my desires and dreams at Your feet, and I surrender myself to You. Forgive all my sins. Replace my fears with faith. Fill me afresh and anew with Your Holy Spirit. Grow the fruit of the Spirit in my life and empower me to advance Your agenda. Lord Jesus, have Your way in me and through me. Amen."

---

[126] PreceptAustin.org @ Romans 15:13

Chapter 26: Interpreting the Book of Acts

The Book of Acts is essentially a history book. But it is more.

So, why did I major in history if I, like most students, viewed it as boring, irrelevant, and a waste of time?

Here is how it happened ...

During the opening weeks of my freshman year at Trinity College, I met with Dr. Vos, the academic advisor assigned to me. He asked, "What do you think you will do after you graduate?" I had no idea. Some students enter college with clear goals, and others, like myself, tend to "drift" from one event in life to the next. "I don't know," I replied. "Maybe I will go to seminary." To this day I have no idea why I said that, other than that it must have been the unseen hand of God guiding me toward His purposes for my life. "Then," replied Dr. Vos, "You should major in history, philosophy, or literature because when you get to seminary, you will get plenty of Bible." Since he was the head of the history department, I chose to major in history. To this day I know very little about history. Nevertheless, I do not regret that I chose that major because I learned an important skill that I have used throughout life; namely, how to research and write.

Acts: Descriptive? or Prescriptive?

The New Testament Book of Acts is an "excellent example of Hellenistic historiography."[127] Historiography is not written simply to record past events but to communicate a point. In the Book of Acts, Dr. Luke's point pertains to the unstoppable progress of the gospel from its Jewish roots in Jerusalem to the Gentile world in Rome, and beyond. Barriers fell and the gospel advanced as the Holy Spirit worked powerfully through key individuals such as Peter, Stephen, Philip, Barnabas, and Paul.

Scholars debate about how to apply the Book of Acts in our day. If Acts is merely descriptive – that is, if it simply describes what happened – then it is more a matter for historians. However, if the Book of Acts goes beyond describing what happened to them then, to prescribing what ought to happen to us now – to every convert and every church in every generation and in every culture – then it is absolutely vital that we understand and apply its prescription to our lives. Dr. Mark Strauss suggests that one of the keys to determining which aspects of Acts are for us today is to look for consistent patterns and repetition.[128] One-time events, such as casting lots (Acts 1:23-26), are not intended to be normative for the church today. In comparison, repeated patterns, such as the Holy Spirit's guidance and empowerment, are for today.

Viewing the Book of Acts as both descriptive per prescriptive led to an "ah-ha!" moment in my life. It became astonishingly clear that empowerment by the Holy Spirit is, in fact, a dominant theme in the New Testament. Receiving the Holy Spirit for salvation was good but it was not good enough. In each case God saw to it that empowerment (i.e., baptism with the Holy Spirit) followed salvation.

---

[127] Gordon Fee and Douglas Stuart, *How to Read the Bible for all Its Worth* (Grand Rapids: Zondervan, 2003), 109.

[128] Mark L. Strauss, *How to Read the Bible in Changing Times* (Grand Rapids: Baker Books, 2011), 177.

We tend to think, "Hallelujah! They accepted Christ. Add a little discipleship and that's all they need." But in Acts, Jesus always orchestrated one more step, namely baptism with the Holy Spirit.

Viewing Acts as both descriptive and prescriptive requires us to emphasize both salvation and empowerment.

Chapter 27: Those Troublesome Tongues

My father instilled into my thinking that all tongues-speaking is of the devil. Further, the Scofield Bible used by every "good" church in my little world during my formative years declared that the sign gifts, including tongues, ceased with the close of the New Testament canon at the end of the first century AD. Suffice it to say that I had no interest in that gift for myself; in fact, I guarded against it. At the same time, I was intrigued by it. On a couple occasions during my 20s and 30s, following long conversation with trusted friends who spoke in tongues, they asked if they could pray for me to receive this gift. I said, "Yes," … but nothing happened.

By the time I began to be involved in Dunamis, my theological understanding of the sign gifts had changed. Through the systematic study of Scripture, I came to the settled conviction that there are legitimate expressions in our day of all the gifts mentioned in Scripture including tongues, healing, prophecy, and miracles. There are also abuses. In a private conversation with Jesus, I told Him that I was open to all the gifts of the Spirit including tongues; but I wanted the real thing, no counterfeits.

During the initial Dunamis conference that I attended in 2000, Victor Matthews prayed for me, saying, "And Jesus, if he does not have the gift of tongues, give it to him." Nothing happened.

A year later, following a teaching on the spiritual gift of tongues, Bill asked who wanted to receive it. I raised my hand; so did several others. People gathered around each of us to pray. I waited quietly and patiently before the Lord as they prayed, sensing His presence but not receiving this gift. Others did. Later that year, Ellen, Julie, and others prayed that same basic prayer for me. Nothing happened.

A year later, much to my joy and surprise, while engaged in exalted worship, my tongue began to "flutter" spontaneously, as if being controlled by a force beyond me; yet, no sounds came forth.

A few years later (May, 2004) I recorded this in my journal:

> Once again, while involved in intense prayer ministry, I found myself praying "silently" in tongues – so intensely that I feared I might not be able to switch back to English! I forced myself to switch back, and have wondered ever since if God might have done more in the life of the person I was praying for if I had stayed longer with the flow of what He was doing.

In November, 2004, I made this notation:

> During the last few months God has been giving me a greater release of the gift of tongues – an odd sort of tongues, I might add. No audible words. Rather, an occasional involuntary fluttering of the tongue during a time of worship or prayer. Sometimes it lasts for a moment; other times, it is sustained. Sometimes it is peaceful; other times, a tempest.

To this day, I am not able to pray in tongues whenever I choose to do so. Many people I know can, but I cannot. Why? I believe that Jesus is honoring my earlier desire for the "real thing" and not some counterfeit. Rarely do I find myself saying anything out loud in tongues; nevertheless, I definitely know when the gift is flowing. For example, while participating in a retreat, I served on one of the prayer teams. One of the ways that the Holy Spirit signals that He is at work within me and preparing me for a time of ministry is through the release of "silent tongues" during worship. By this I mean that my tongue begins to flutter almost uncontrollably – sometimes intensely as if engaging in battle. I am "speaking" but no sounds are coming forth. During the worship time prior to our prayer ministry, the Spirit was "chattering" within me intensely. This manifestation of the Spirit continued throughout the next hour as my prayer partner and I prayed for people

In 2013, while waiting in the front row to speak at another church, I watched an Asian sister lead worship in a manner that was genuine, fervent, and joyful. I sensed that the Lord was giving her prophetic words to share with the congregation but she was holding back. Following my teaching on "Being Led By The Spirit" (Romans 8:14), I shared with her (in the presence of her pastor) what I was sensing. She affirmed that that was indeed the case but she did not know what to do with the words she was hearing. I asked her if she would like me to pray for her. "Yes!" Then I asked her pastor's permission to pray for her. "Yes." I placed my hands on her head and began to pray in English. After a few moments, I paused to listen for the Spirit's guidance. The Spirit fell upon me, and I began to speak in tongues as my hands remained on her head. I felt, and heard, the Holy Spirit surging powerfully, yet gently, deep within me for her. "How long will this last?" I wondered. Not knowing the answer and being a time-conscious person, I almost interrupted the flow; however, I chose to wait and let it continue. After a couple of minutes, the Spirit's surging dissipated as He lifted. We concluded the time of ministry by anointing her with oil and, in the name of the Father, Son, and

Holy Spirit, sealing what God had done during that time of prayer in her life.

Later that week, she emailed and asked about the content of my prayer. "I don't know," I replied, "because it was in tongues. However, since God is good, I'm sure it was good. Just receive by saying, 'Jesus, thank You for what You are doing in my life.'"

Four Kinds of Tongues

While attending a conference for pastors, a few of us met informally during a coffee break. In the process of telling us about a new church in his area that was growing like a weed, George observed, "But I do not think they are a Biblical church. For example, they permit people to speak in tongues during their worship services but no one interprets. According to 1 Corinthians 14, tongues are supposed to be interpreted."

For years, I, too, held the view that every expression of the spiritual gift of tongues must be interpreted, and I based this view on Paul's instructions to the Church in Corinth:

> *Therefore, one who speaks in a tongue should pray that he may interpret. ... 27 If any speak in a tongue, let there be only two or at most three, and each in turn, <u>and let someone interpret</u>. 28 But if there is no one to interpret, let each of them keep silent in church and speak to himself and to God.* 1 Corinthians 14:13,27,28, ESV

In his book, *The Walk of the Spirit – The Walk of Power*, Dave Roberson challenged me to go back to Scripture and take a closer look at the contexts in which the spiritual gift of tongues is mentioned. Although several aspects of Roberson's exegesis are weak, I believe that he is on track when he identifies four kinds of tongues in the New Testament.[129] Briefly, they are:

1. Tongues for personal edification, often called a "prayer language."

> *The one who speaks in a tongue builds up himself.*
> 1 Corinthians 14:4, ESV

Our prayer ministry team experienced this kind of tongues following a worship service. A young lady approached us and requested prayer. Gathering around her, we asked permission to rest our hands on her shoulders. Then, some of the team's members began praying … in tongues … all together at once. After a few minutes, we began praying in English.

Why did the prayer team begin by praying in tongues? Three reasons:

- To focus their hearts and minds on God. By praying in tongues we turn our hearts toward God. *One who speaks in a tongue speaks not to men but to God,* 1 Corinthians 14:2a, ESV.

- To be built up spiritually. When we pray in tongues, we acknowledge that we lack the resources needed for the ministry at hand. We invite the Holy Spirit to build us up (1 Corinthians 14:4) and equip us to advance the Father's will for that person at that time.

---

[129] See A.T. Robertson, *Robertson's Word Pictures of the New Testament* (Broadman Press, 1932, 1933), 86f.

- To step into the stream of what God is doing. Running ahead of the Spirit will do no good; neither will lagging behind Him. Praying in tongues is a way of wading into the stream of His work, and flowing with Him. When we are aligned with Him, His work gets done. Jesus is glorified and we experience the joy that comes to those who partner with Him.

In this case, did their expressions of tongues need to be interpreted? No, because no one was giving a <u>message</u> in tongues; they were merely doing what Scripture gives us permission to do; namely, to speak in tongues in order to build ourselves up.

During a ministry prayer time for an individual, God gave me the presence of mind to set the stage by saying,

> We are going to invite Jesus to draw near and minister. Please be comfortable with times of silence as we listen to God for guidance. You, too, are welcome to join in and offer a prayer during this time.

As we waited together in silence, tongues began to flow within me and I sensed God giving me discernment regarding what He was doing in that individual's life. As I spoke forth these impressions in English, the recipient's nonverbal responses indicated that the words were touching his heart. During that entire ministry time, I sensed the authority of the King quietly and powerfully at work.

Who doesn't need to be built up?!? Speaking in tongues is one of many tools that Jesus has given us to strengthen ourselves spiritually so that we are better equipped to face life.

Even though interpretation is not essential in these instances, on occasion Jesus gives it. For example, following a conversation with one of the ladies whom God called to intercede for me, she asked if she could pray over me in tongues. I said, "Yes," and she did. Beautiful; very touching. Even though I did not understand a word she said, the Spirit's presence was palpable. Then, she interpreted what she heard the Lord saying. "Don't worry about John and Sheri." A moment later, "I have anointed you. Believe. Do not be afraid." The Lord's words through her enabled me to minister with greater confidence during the evening session.[130]

2. Tongues that need to be interpreted.

My first experience of tongues and interpretation occurred many years ago while my family and I were on vacation in Florida. We happened to attend a large church with Charismatic leanings. During the worship service, the leaders encouraged the congregation to offer to God expressions of worship. Everyone lifted their voice in praise, some speaking or singing in English; others, in tongues. It was beautiful! After a few minutes of this glorious offering of praise, the whole congregation quieted, as if being directed by an unseen orchestra conductor. Following a brief pause, one person raised his voice and spoke in tongues. Once again I thought, "How beautiful!" A few moments later, from the other side of the room, another person spoke up and interpreted what the tongues-speaker had just said. At that time, the whole experience was totally foreign to me; yet, it seemed so right, fitting, harmonious, and God-honoring ... because, as I have come to learn, it was.

What we witnessed was a message in tongues, and when a message in tongues is given, the Bible calls for an

---

[130] The gift of tongues is not the evidence that we have been baptized with the Holy Spirit; rather, it is one of several possible indicators. See 1 Corinthians 12:7-11.

258

interpretation. At that church service, scores of people were speaking in tongues, but only one needed interpretation.

> *If any speak in a tongue, let there be only two or at most three, and each in turn, <u>and let someone interpret</u>. But if there is no one to interpret, let each of them keep silent in church and speak to himself and to God.* 1 Corinthians 14:27-28, ESV

In 2013, Teri and I had the privilege of traveling with a small group to Israel. Traditionally, people who visit the Western Wall in Jerusalem write a prayer on a scrap of paper, and place it in a crack in the Wall. The prayer that bubbled up within me as I approached the Wall was:

> "Fire! Lord, let your fire fall on your servant! Consume the dross and empower your servant with Holy Spirit fire to do Your work and impact nations."

Two hours later while at the Holy Sepulcher following Communion, the Lord released a message in tongues through a Christian sister and an interpretation through another. I knew intuitively that it was for me. As I listened, the Holy Spirit drew near – very, very near to my heart – and tears welled up from deep within. The general thrust of the interpretation, which twice included the word "fire" and twice the phrase "resurrection power," was this:

> Jesus is the resurrection and the life and He is releasing resurrection power – fresh fire upon you to do what He is calling you to do. He will empower you with resurrection power to carry His Word from this place to the ends of the earth.

3. Tongues for deep intercession.

During seasons of intense need, the Holy Spirit may move people to travail in prayer, speaking in their prayer language. On these occasions, interpretation is not necessary because Jesus understands the "language" perfectly. Paul told the Romans:

> *Likewise, the Spirit helps us in our weakness. For we do not know what to pray for as we ought, but the Spirit himself intercedes for us with <u>groanings too deep for words</u>.* Romans 8:26, ESV

On several occasions, including a recent mission trip to Uganda, Africa, I have witnessed intercessors engaged in travailing prayer. Their entire being expresses the prayer. Sometimes they look and sound like they are giving birth. God uses travailing prayers to shape the future.

4. Tongues for evangelism.

Although I have never had this experience, several people have told me stories about times when they were attempting to share the gospel with someone who spoke another language. Suddenly they heard themselves speaking in tongues, and as they did, the other person answered in the same language. Why? Because their expression of tongues was a known language, namely, the other person's language.[131]

Apparently, that is what happened on the Day of Pentecost:

---

[131] See stories in Dave Roberson, *The Walk of the Spirit – The Walk of Power* (Tulsa, OK: Dave Roberson Ministries, 1999), 99-104.

> *And they were all filled with the Holy Spirit and began to speak in other tongues as the Spirit gave them utterance. 5 Now there were dwelling in Jerusalem Jews, devout men from every nation under heaven. 6 And at this sound the multitude came together, and they were bewildered, because each one was <u>hearing them speak in his own language</u>.* Acts 2:4-6, ESV

On the Day of Pentecost, Jesus, through the Holy Spirit, enabled the Apostles to speak in languages that they had never learned but that were known to people gathered in the diverse crowd in Jerusalem for the celebration Pentecost.[132] Net result: many came to faith in Jesus Christ.

Summation

The gift of tongues, like every gift that Jesus gives, is a good gift. Let's take Jude's exhortation to heart:

> *But you, beloved, <u>building yourselves up</u> in your most holy faith and <u>praying in the Holy Spirit</u>, keep yourselves in the love of God, waiting for the mercy of our Lord Jesus Christ that leads to eternal life.* Jude 1:20-21, ESV

---

[132] I understand that some say it was a miracle of hearing. In either case, the God used tongues to do the work of evangelism.

For Further Reflection

Chapter 22: Baptized with the Holy Spirit at Conversion?

1. What have you been taught about the meaning of 1 Corinthians 12:13?

2. Reflect on your life and describe:

   a. The regenerating work of the Holy Spirit in your life

   b. The empowering work of the Holy Spirit in your life

Chapter 23: Critique of Cessationism

1. What objections might a Cessationist raise in response to this chapter?

2. Agree or Disagree: People who are Cessationists and people who are Charismatics:
   a. can live together peacefully in the same family
   b. can work together closely in the same church

Chapter 24: The Dual Meaning of "Filled"

1. In your own words, summarize the main points of this chapter and discuss its relevance for you and for us.

2. In addition to our call to serve as witnesses, what is your understanding of your mission? Invite the others in the group to lay hands on you and pray for a fresh infilling with the Holy Spirit, equipping you to fulfill Jesus' calling on your life.

Chapter 26: Those Troublesome Tongues?

1. What is your story? What has been your experience with tongues? What comments or questions do you have about tongues?

2. Would you like someone to lay hands on you, and join you in inviting Jesus to bless you with this spiritual gift?

Chapter 28: Receive Your Torch

The "dance of cooperation" with the Father, Son, and Holy Spirit is elevated to new levels when we are baptized with the Holy Spirit.

We can shut Him down. Or, we can step out onto the dance floor and thrive!

- Receive the Holy Spirit "within" for new life and transformation.

- Receive the Holy Spirit "upon" for the release of greater power for witness and service.

Recently John Zhang, an electrical engineer who is also a dynamic prayer warrior, shared a vision that God gave him in 2005. As I listened I thought, "This vision is not only for John, but also for many, many others." Here is what John "saw":

> I saw a large ring of fire descending from the dark sky. It stopped and was hovering before and above me. I went up and noticed that the giant ring of fire was composed of many individual torches. I knew that I was being invited and encouraged to take a torch off the ring. Even though torches were constantly being taken off the ring by many people, the ring of fire

miraculously remained the same: I did not see any vacant positions at any time. Each person, after taking a torch, would hold it high and run into the darkness. I took a torch and ran into the darkness. As I did I could clearly see dotted lines of lights from other torches winding into the fields. All the while the giant ring of fire hovered steadily in the sky, accessible to others also.

Receive your torch ... and run into the darkness! The Holy Spirit is the *FireStarter*.

About the Author

I am a follower of Jesus Christ who has tasted the goodness of God and the powers of the age to come and hungers for more.

After graduating from Wheaton College in 1972 with a BA in History, I enrolled in Fuller Theological Seminary, Pasadena, CA, and graduated in 1975 with a M.Div. (Master of Divinity). In the early 1990s I returned to Fuller to work on my D.Min. (Doctorate of Ministry). Following a delightful journey – really, I loved it! - I graduated in 1997. Hence, my formal title is Rev. Dr. Philip J. Noordmans.

Since 1975, I have served in a variety of pastoral and teaching roles in the Midwest and in California. Currently I am serving part-time as a Regional Pastor.

I thank God for His grace and endeavor to continue growing deeper in intimacy with the Father, Son, and Holy Spirit.

Phil and Teri in China, 2015

Bibliography

Agnew, Milton S. "The Holy Spirit - Friend and Counselor."
Christianity Today, n.d.

Banister, Doug. *The Word and Power Church.* Grand Rapids,
MI: Zondervan, 1999.

Barrett, C.K. *A Commentary on the First Epistle to the
Corinthians.* New York: Harper & Row, 1968.

Bauer, Arndt, and Gingrich. *A Greek-English Lexicon of the
New Testament and Other Early Christian Literature.*
Chicago: University of Chicago Press, 1971.

Bennett, Dennis. *The Holy Spirit and You.* North Brunswick,
NJ: Bridge-Logos Publishers, 1971.

Brown, Colin. "The New International Dictionary of New
Testament Theology." Fourth Printing, Oct. 1979.

Brown; Driver; Briggs. *Hebrew and English Lexicon of the Old
Testament.* Oxford: Clarendon Press, 1974.

Carson, D.A. *Showing the Spirit: A Theological Exposition of 1
Corinthians 12-14.* Grand Rapids, MI: Baker Book
House: Baker Book House, Fourth Printing, July 1992.

Chambers, Oswald. *My Utmost for His Highest.* Uhrichsville,
OH : Barbour and Company, Inc., 1963.

Chan, Francis and Sprinkle, Preston. *Erasing Hell.* David
Cook, 2011.

Cho, David (Paul) Yonggi. *The Fourth Dimension.* Seoul,
Korea: Seoul Logos Co., Inc., 1979.

Clark, Randy. *Baptism in the Holy Spirit.* Global Awakening,
2011.

Concordance, Strong's Exhaustive.
*http://www.biblestudytools.com/concordances/strongs-
exhaustive-concordance/.* n.d.

Constable, Thomas.
    http://www.soniclight.com/constable/notes/. n.d.
Dana, H.E, and Mantey, Julius R. *A Manual Grammar of the
    Greek New Testament.* The MacMillan Company, 1927,
    40th printing 1955.
Deere, Jack. *Surprised by the Power of the Spirit.* Grand
    Rapids, MI: Zondervan, 1993.
English Standard Version Study Bible. Wheaton, IL: Crossway
    Bibles, 2008.
Fee, Gordon and Stuart, Douglas. *How to Read the Bible for
    All Its Worth.* Grand Rapids: Zondervan, 2003.
Foster, Richard J. *Celebration of Discipline.* n.d.
Green, Craig. "A Fresh Method." *Charisma Magazine,*
    December 2012: 50.
Green, Michael. *I Believe in the Holy Spirit.* Grand Rapids:
    Eerdmans, 1977.
Grudem, Wayne. *Systematic Theology.* Grand Rapids, MI:
    Zondervan, 1994.
Hummel, Charles E. *Fire in the Fireplace.* Downers Grove, IL:
    InterVarsity Press, Second Edition 1979.
Jeremiah, David. *God in You.* Sisters, Oregon: Multnomah
    Publishers, 1998.
Keillor, Garrison. "My Five Most Important Books."
    Newsweek Magazine, December 24, 2007: 17.
Kendall, R.T. "They Cease to Believe." *Charisma Magazine,*
    2014 йил February: 42.
Long, Brad. *The Healing Ministry of Jesus.* prmi.org, n.d.
Long, Brad; McMurry, Douglas. *Gateways to Empowered
    Ministry.* The Dunamis Project, prmi.org, Revised
    2006.
Long, Brad; Stokes, Paul; Strickler, Cindy. *Growing the
    Church in the Power of the Holy Spirit.* Grand Rapids,
    MI: Zondervan, 2009.
Long, Zeb Bradford, and McMurry, Douglas. *Receiving the
    Power.* Grand Rapids, MI: Chosen Books / Baker Book
    House, 1996.

MacNutt, Francis. *Deliverance from Evil Spirits.* Grand
　　Rapids, MI: Choosen Books, 1995.

—. "My Search for the Spirit." *HealingLine*, Spring 2014.

Marshall, Catherine. *The Helper.* Avon Books, 1978.

Marshall, I. Howard. *The Acts of the Apostles.* Grand Rapids,
　　MI: Eerdmans, Reprinted 1987.

Moreland, J P. *Kingdom Triangle.* Grand Rapids, MI:
　　Zondervan, 2007.

Morris, Leon. *The Gospel According to John.* Grand Rapids,
　　MI: Eerdmans Publishing Co., Reprinted 1981.

Net Bible. https://net.bible.org, n.d.

NIV Study Bible. Grand Rapids, MI: Zondervan, 1985.

Packer, J.I. *Keep In Step With the Spirit.* Baker Books, 2005.

Perry, Michele. "Supernatural Myth-Busters." *Charisma
　　Magazine*, May 2013: 61.

Pollock, J.C. *A Biographical Portrait of the Pacesetter in
　　Modern Mass Evangelism.* New York: MacMillan,
　　1963.

PreceptAustin. "http://preceptaustin.org." n.d.

Reformation Study Bible (ESV). Orlando, FL: Ligonier
　　Ministries. R.C. Sproul, General Editor, 2005.

Rienecker, Fritz; and Rogers, Jr., Cleon. *Linguistic Key to the
　　Greek New Testament.* Grand Rapids, MI: Regency
　　Reference Library: Zondervan, 1980.

Roberson, Dave. *The Walk of the Spirit - The Walk of Power.*
　　Tulsa, OK: Dave Roberson Ministries, 1999.

Robertson, A. T. *Robertson's Word Pictures of the New
　　Testament.* http://www.studylight.org/com/rwp/:
　　Broadman Press, 1932,33, Renewal 1960.

Sproul, R.C. *Essential Truths of the Christian Faith.* Wheaton,
　　IL: Tyndale House Publishers, Inc, 1992.

Storm, Sam. "Strange Fire and the Cessationist Attack."
　　Chaisma Magazine, 2014: 49-50.

Stott, John R.W. *Baptism & Fullness: The Work of the Holy
　　Spirit Today.* Downers Grove, IL: InterVarsity Press,
　　Second Edition, 1975.

Strauss, Mark L. *How to Read the Bible in Changing Times.* Grand Rapids, MI: Baker Books, 2011.

Strong, James. *Strong's Exhaustive Concordance of the Bible.* See http://biblehub.com/strongs.htm, 1890.

Synan, Vinson. *The Holiness-Pentecostal Tradition: Charismatic Movements in the Twentieth Century.* Eerdmans, 1997.

Torrey, R. A. *The Holy Spirit: Who He Is and What He Does.* Edited by P.O. Box 279, Seelyville, IN, 47878 Herald of His Coming. Classic Books for Today, NO. 152., 2000.

—. *The Person and Work of the Holy Spirit.* Grand Rapids, MI: Zondervan, 1910; 1974.

Torrey, R.A. *Power-Filled Living.* New Kensington, PA: Whitaker House, 1999.

—. *What the Bible Teaches About the Holy Spirit.* New York, NY: Revel, 1898.

Tozer, A.W. *How to be Filled with the Holy Spirit.* Harrisburg, PA: Christian Publications, n.d.

—. "Tozer on the Holy Spirit." *A 366-day Devotional Compiled by Marilynne E. Foster.* 2007.

Watson, David. *I Believe in the Church.* Grand Rapids: Wm. B. Eerdmans, 1979.

Williams, Don. *Signs, Wonders, and the Kingdom of God.* Vine Books, ISBN 0-89283-602-4, 1989.

Wood, George O. "Marks of the Assemblies." *Charisma Magazine,* August 2014: 34.

Yoars, Marcus. "10 Revolutions for the New Year." *Charisma Magazine,* 2013: 6.

Books by Philip J. Noordmans

Available on Amazon.com in paper back and/or Kindle ebook

FireStarter: The Holy Spirit Empowers

FireStarter combines deeply personal stories and careful exegesis to chronicle my journey from laboring as a dispensational cessationist to living as a grateful, balanced charismatic. 265 pages. $12.95 / $4.95

A Primer on the Empowering Work of the Holy Spirit

Real people. Compelling stories. Clear teaching on the Person and work of the Holy Spirit.

Whereas *FireStarter* weaves stories from my life into teaching about the empowering work of the Holy Spirit, *A Primer on the Empowering Work of the Holy Spirit* intertwines teaching with stories of the Holy Spirit's work in the lives of others.

A primer (prim-er) is a small, introductory book on a subject, and in this case the subject is the empowering work of the Holy Spirit. This booklet does not promote showmanship, sensationalism, or mindless faith; rather, it lays a solid, biblical foundation for a relationship with the Holy Spirit that is real, personal, and dynamic. 110 pages. $7.00 / $3.00

Holy Spirit Course

Twelve lessons about the empowering work of the Holy Spirit. Includes outlines that may be duplicated. 131 pages. $10.00 / $3.00

A Primer on Spiritual Gifts

Fresh insights for a new generation on the timeless topic of spiritual gifts.

A Primer [Prim-er] on Spiritual Gifts merges careful scholarship with real-life stories to help you identify, develop, and deploy your spiritual gifts for the glory of God and the common good. Soon you will be serving in ways that replenish your joy and advance our King's agenda.

Save yourself the trouble of filling out spiritual gift tests and tabulating results in databases. A thoughtful reading of this material will open the eyes of your heart to your God-given, Holy Spirit energized spiritual strengths, as well as to the gifts of others. Ideal for individual or group study. 151 pages. $9.00 / $3.50

> I read the *Primer on Spiritual Gifts* and found it to be the very best writings on God's equipping (gifting) His people to live the Kingdom way of life. I plan to use it for part two of a study I am doing on "Kingdom Living" developed through the Praxis Center for Church Development. Thank you for listening to the

Holy Spirit and writing a great easy-to-read book on
spiritual giftings.
Dean Walker, Educator, Pastor

Uncovering the Heart and Truth of Scripture: Gleaning Meaning from God's Word

Is what that verse means to you what it really means?

Every student of Scripture and every teacher of Scripture will
benefit from this easy-to-read introduction to hermeneutics,
which is the art and science of interpreting Scripture. Better
Bible study helps. 111 pages. $5.95 / $2.95

Why Pray? Because Sometimes God Relents!

In addition to wrestling with the meaning of "God relents," this
booklet offers timeless insights into the mystery of prayer. The
illustrations will add courage to beleaguered pray-ers.
25 pages. $4.95 / $2.50

The End: Charity Tracker and the Last Dance

For years I have questioned the pre-tribulation rapture
perspective behind publications such as the *Left Behind* series.
This captivating novel builds on a wiser eschatological
bedrock, one that encourages believers to anticipate and
prepare for hard times ahead.

The appendices are worth their weight in gold in that they
utilize bullet points and diagrams to summarize stepping stones
to the end. 88 pages. $7.00 / $2.50

The Kingdom of God: From Near to Here: Four Stages of Kingdom Development

This book includes Biblical and practical insights into the four stages of Kingdom development hidden in plain sight in the pages of Scripture. In addition it includes a definition of the Kingdom of God that emerged from an "ah-ha" moment in the gospels. Seeing these stages will provide answers to many of the real-life tensions we experience on a daily basis, including the problem of evil. 67 pages. $7.00 / $2.95

Each of Phil's books is **available on Amazon** as a paperback and eBook. *Please take a moment to leave a review.* These books have not been professionally edited: you will find a few typos. For bulk discounts you may contact me at
pnoordmans12@gmail.com,
2136 Chennault Ave., Clovis, CA, 93611; 858-231-6353

Soli Deo Gloria